S0-CFH-123

Grumbles
From The Keyboard

Or

How I Learned To Stop Worrying and Love My Computer.

Courtland Nederveld

Copyright © 2011 Courtland Nederveld

Turning Crank Publishing

Punta Gorda, FL

All rights reserved.

No part of this book or its content may be reproduced in any form, or by any electronic, mechanical or other means, without permission in writing from the publisher.

ISBN-10: 1467985899
ISBN-13: 978-1467985895

DEDICATION

For Peggy Nederveld

Computers are good at following instructions, but not at reading your mind.
Donald Knuth

Grumbles From The Keyboard
www.grumblesfromthekeyboard.com

Additional Titles by Courtland Nederveld

Epicuria
Adventures That Really Cook!
www.myepicuria.com

CONTENTS

ACKNOWLEDGMENTS

To Gordon Bower Retired Editor, Punta Gorda Herald, for suggesting the column in 2004. To Peggy Nederveld, for her encouragement and editing of the columns over the years. To the Charlotte Sun Herald Newspapers that carries the column each week. To Martha, unflinchingly serving the role of muse, foil and good sport. To Dominic Cretacci who contributed "Your Computer can make you a star." Finally, to the readers who lent their questions, suggestions, comments and support over the years.

Cover Illustration and Design
Val Heisey

GRUMBLES FROM THE KEYBOARD

OR
HOW I LEARNED TO STOP WORRYING AND LOVE MY COMPUTER

Grumbles from the Keyboard is a collection of newspaper columns written over a period of six years. Published as *Bits and Bytes,* under the Court Nederveld byline, the column appears each Wednesday in the Charlotte Sun. The column is written for the average home computer user, mom and dad, grandma and grandpa and those folks that do not consider themselves techno geeks.

Over the years several things occurred. First, technology changes at a frightening pace. If I considered that I might eventually cover all topics and have nothing more to write about, technological advances provided an endless stream of new column ideas. While constructing this anthology, I reviewed over three hundred columns and found some referencing topics or products that are no longer relevant or no longer exist. Second, many computer users harbor a fear of computers because they seems so mysterious. The columns attempted to inject a bit of humor into human/computer relationships simply to allow people to take a deep breath and realize that it really isn't as frightening as it seems. Third, the folks that I deal with on a day to day basis use a tiny portion of the potential built into not only the PC, but its connection to the Internet as well. If I could demonstrate the enormous power, knowledge and utility of these calculating constructs, they may begin to embrace all the benefits available to even the most non-technical user.

When outlining Grumbles From The Keyboard, it seemed to take on a life of its own. Certainly, the tome would contain many of the columns pertinent to computer use and maintenance. But to simply reprint old columns seemed redundant. New and never published pieces are included where relevant.

Finally, the weekly Bits and Bytes column was constrained to seven hundred words while running in the weekly inserts and trimmed to five hundred words when the column moved to the front section of the paper. Sometimes there were additional points that were salient to the theme but left on the cutting room floor because of length. As each column was reviewed and vetted for inclusion in Grumbles From The Keyboard, I took the liberty of adding to a column if the information seemed relevant and updated where necessary. Consequently some of the chapters will be longer than the column was when originally published.

Like many of my readers, there are grandkids involved in my life. Unlike many readers, these grandkids are a bit reluctant to challenge Opa's knowledge of things that use binary code. It really bugs the little rug rats when Opa turns out to be smarter than they are. Because it elicits a chuckle to see the ankle biters trying to figure out how this old geezer knows this stuff, I decided to provide readers with a vocabulary building program through out the book. Within each chapter there will be a computer or Internet related word or phrase printed in bold type. At the bottom of the page will be a box labeled "Grandpa and Grandma, how come you're so smart??" In this box will be the bold word, its definition and a couple of sentences that demonstrate how to use it.

Another column favorite over the years were the comments by Martha. Those familiar with the column know that Martha, in her own way, simply said what most of us were silently thinking. With Grumbles From The Keyboard, Martha is invited to offer a bit more than her usual one liners.

Grumbles From The Keyboard is grouped by topic, so columns will not appear in chronological order. As a desk side reference putting similar or related columns together will make it easier to find information as needed. As of the completion of the book December of 2011 all the website addresses listed were active.

Every book needs to start somewhere. Grumbles from the Keyboard will start with a column published, June 6th, 2005 which emphasizes that our calculating construct is nothing more than a tool designed to make our lives easier.

Enjoy!

Courtland Nederveld

IT'S JUST A TOOL

Tools. Everyone has some. A hammer is a tool for building things. A spatula is a tool for cooking. A light switch is a tool for controlling illumination. Even the remote control is a tool for preventing over exertion. Whatever type of tool it is, it is designed to help you do more with less energy and get the job done faster. Some tools are multi talented. The hammer can also serve as a pry bar. The spatula was used as a corrective action tool by my parents. And of course the remote control is a conversation starter between my wife and I. (Click that remote ONE more time…..)

Now look at that bright and shiny new **computer** sitting in the corner. I want you to say to yourself, "this is nothing more than a tool." Now keep repeating that as you read the rest of the column.

First, let's state the obvious. The computer will connect to all your acquaintances via email. It will surf the World Wide Web. It will also let you play solitaire. But there is so much more. Let's see if there is something it can do that will fascinate and amaze. I find that once someone discovers that one thing that interest them, they stop "trying to learn" the computer and start using it to meet their needs.

For example, I recently met a couple that bought their very first computer. They hired me to train them in some of the basics. For over an hour, I walked them through various exercises. They wrote copious notes, diagrams, asked many questions and as the time went by became more and more confused. During this session, we talked about different things and one of the topics that interested them was property appraisals and taxes. I decided to use www.ccapraiser.com as a lesson topic. I had to smile, as they perused the tax records and maps available on this site, they were doing all the things I had tried to teach them in the last hour, without once looking at their pages of notes. Even more interesting, I had them shut down the computer. Then I simply asked them to go back to the county appraiser's site and look up some piece of information. They never looked at their notes; they turned on the machine, went to the Internet, typed in the URL and then navigated their way around the site.

Grandma and Grandpa, how come you're so smart?
Computer: An electronic device designed to accept data, perform prescribed mathematical and logical operations and display the results of these operations.
I used a computer to purchase airline tickets on the web.
My computer helps me keep track of my finances.
Wrong: I didn't just fall off the turnip truck; I have been using computers since the Civil War.

They will use the computer because they want to, not because someone "learned" them. One gentleman I spoke with told me that he pays all his bills online. He uses a service called Bill Pay that his bank provides. Five minutes is all it takes for him to pay all his bills for the month. No writing checks, no stamps, no envelopes, no checks lost or stolen. Thinking of starting a business? A client of mine needed a 440-volt distribution panel for his manufacturing plant. He got a quote for a new one from a local electrical company for $12000 plus the breaker that had to go with it. My client went to www.ebay.com and bought a nearly new panel with the breaker and delivered to his facility for $2500.

How about research? I threw a 50th anniversary party for my parents a while back and decided that it would be interesting to know the top ten songs for the year they were married. I not only found the top ten, but also found a CD put out by RCA a decade ago that had the top twenty songs from that year digitally re-mastered for only ten dollars. It was a hit at the party. Another client has hundreds of years of his family's genealogy, which he has gleaned from online records.

Do you have an opinion? Want to share it with thousands of other people? There are thousands of chat rooms, blogs, (web logs) and of course Facebook, MySpace, Google Plus. Picasa, Windows Live Photos, Shutterfly, and Snapfish among many other sites, allow us to share our photographic masterpieces with friends and family. Instant messaging systems such as Skype, Messenger, AIM and more, allow us to communicate with people anywhere in the world both by voice and video at little or no cost. Speaking of anywhere in the world, I use the Internet to play chess against people around the globe. I have played against people in New Zealand, Argentina, England and lots of other places.

The easiest way to learn the capabilities of the computer is to find something that you are interested in. A hobby, shopping, a project or just trying to improve your knowledge will make you forget about "learning" and suck you into doing. Yes, you can use a computer.

Say it again with me. This is nothing more than a tool.

OLD COMPUTERS ARE FILLING THE HOUSE

Let me see a show of hands. How many people have at least one old computer on a shelf in the garage, in a closet, or stashed in the attic? Let me ask you a question. Do you really believe that Windows 3.1 is going to return? Is it possible people will tire of CD-ROMs, DVDs or USB pocket drives and will come begging for your old five and a half inch floppies? I know that some of you, and you know who you are, actually have an old Windows 95 machine set up for the grandkids. Shame on you! Why don't you just give the grandkids a stick and an old iron hoop to push around the living room? Who among you still likes to surf the web on that blazing fast 14400 modem?

All right you say, "I need to break with the past." But, it is so hard to let go of that overwhelming 8 megs of memory. Do you fondly recall when your new computer arrived boasting an unheard of 640 megs of storage on the **hard-drive**? You promptly put half of that storage in your will for the kids because there wasn't that much information in the entire world. It is hard to believe that an entire sixteen years has passed since the release of Windows 95. What's that you say? Your PC is running Windows 98? Did you know that since Windows 98 there has been Windows ME, Windows 2000 Windows XP, Windows Vista and now, my favorite Windows 7?

Now that you have come face to face with the reality of the situation, the question is what to do with this wonderful but useless machine?

Sell it on EBay! Wait a minute, if you don't want it, why would anybody else? Well, the truth is, nobody wants it. I have tried selling parts from old machines thinking that people in third world counties would eat this stuff up just like the carrots and broccoli my mom always said they were starving for in China. Fact is, most computers are made over there and they get them before we do. Consider; they may be sending us their unwanted PCs.

How about donating it to the schools? Let me see, for a few hundred dollars of your tax money the schools buy top of the line, first class, high-speed computers for every room in the school. Yup, the schools will be

Grandma and Grandpa, how come you're so smart?
Hard Drive: A hard drive is a non-volatile, random access digital magnetic data storage device.
The hard-drive in my computer is nearly filled with photos and music.
If the hard-drive should ever fail, I'll be thankful I did regular backups of important files.
Wrong: Timmy, without a map it will be a hard drive back to your mother.

lining up to get their hands on your old, non running PC.

What does that leave? Set it out by the road for trash pickup. Bad idea. If you want to be PC, (that's politically correct not personal computer) then you really don't want to do that. Here is why. The National Safety Council estimates that 63 million computers will become obsolete in 2005. Of these, 75 percent will be stored. (Do you have an extra shelf in the garage?) By 2007 an estimated 500 million machines will need to be disposed of. (How full is your attic?) Each computer contains, in varying amounts, things like plastics, glass, steel, gold, (did he say gold, Martha) lead, mercury, cadmium and fire retardants. If thrown away, these machines release toxins to the environment, polluting the groundwater that comes through our faucets and the air that we breathe.

So what to do? Thankfully, there are ways to recycle these old dinosaurs. For those that want a quick and simple method and you live in Charlotte County, FL., take your non-functioning machines to West Charlotte Mini Transfer Stations located at 7070 Environmental Way in Englewood or 19675 Kenilworth Blvd, Port Charlotte. They will take old PCs and old monitors but only four per year. If you live outside Charlotte County fire up the computer and surf over to http://earth911.com/recycling/electronics/. This site will allow us to plug in our zip code and tell us the nearest places we can recycle electronics. I was surprised at how many retailers offer electronic recycling. Some of them have a small handling charge but at least I know it will be recycled and not end up in a landfill. If your PC is not ancient and still runs, then try some of the local charitable organizations such as Goodwill, Habitat for Humanity and many others. Check with them first as they may have guidelines that explain what they will and will not take. Some of them refurbish, resell or donate to folks that need but can't afford a computer. Let's safely clean out those old PCs and make room for the one in your den. It's already three years old.

DITCHING OLD COMPUTERS

New and shiny. Fast and feature full. Windows 7 seems to be accelerating its capture of the computer user's eye. Many folks are making the move to rotate out their older computers replacing them with new models. Windows XP machines and even a few Vista machines are finding themselves tucked in a corner, stuck in the garage or (GASP) set out by the curb. What have these faithful digital savants done to deserve such an ignominious end? Are they just not fast enough? Sleek enough? Not powerful enough? Are they unable to leapt tall searches with a single click?

Certainly if a **motherboard** bursts, or a hard drive dumps, memory melts or other physical calamity befalls our calculating concubine it is time to put it to rest. The decision to discard comes easy but how should the task be tackled? In Charlotte County there are two ways to leave your electronic mentalist. One is good and one is bad. Choose the one that fits your style. The easiest and bad way is to set it out by the curb. This will ensure that a hundred years from now, someone will find it rusting away in a landfill.

A tiny bit more difficult but certainly much more kind to our world is to take it to a recycling location. Where is that we ask? Suellen McElroy, Program Coordinator, Environmental & Extension Services for Charlotte County, FL reminds us that those wanting a quick and simple method for disposing of electronics, the County recommends taking the Ewaste to the Transfer Facility's at 7070 Environmental Way, Englewood or 19675 Kenilworth Blvd, Port Charlotte. They take old PCs, monitors, keyboards, printers, TV's (small & large), VCR's, stereos, scanners, microwave ovens, copiers, and miscellaneous electronics. The County contracts with Creative Recycling Systems, Inc (www.crserecycling.com) to handle our electronic flotsam.

But what about that computer still processing data, the one that served as our door to the Internet? Don't look to any Charlotte County schools to take our hand me downs. This is the 21st century, every school not only gets the latest and greatest with our tax dollars, but they even have a store where their hand me downs are available for sale to us. There must be some way to allow a useful tool to help someone else. There are two possibilities in Charlotte County that might be a jumping off point for a computer's second life.

> **Grandma and Grandpa, how come you're so smart?**
> **Motherboard** : (mobo) The main printed circuit board a computer.
> The motherboard, like the floor in the house, connects all rooms together.
> My motherboard, also called a system board, requires a specific type of memory module.
> Wrong: Tammy, playing video games all day will really make her motherboard.

The Charlotte County Computer Group Corporation (cccgc.net) is located at the Cultural Center in Port Charlotte, 2280 Aaron Street, Phone (941) 625-4175, ext 244 office hours are 10:00 AM – 2:00 PM M-F.

CCCGC is an authorized Microsoft MAR refurbisher. They repair, rebuild and then provide computers to nearly 300 needy children each year. A functioning or repairable PC would find a good home after receiving the once over to bring it back to fighting strength.

There is still another place to drop off that lively but retired machine that would allow it to serve the function it was designed for. The Family Literacy Center of Charlotte County (surf over to charlottecountyfl.com/HumanServices/FamilyServices) accepts donations of old computers. Professional computer personnel will clear your hard drive and transfer files, if you need assistance with this. The computers are used to teach English to those native to a different language. Contact Holly Rodriguez at the Family Services Center at 941-627-0643.

For those that do not live in Charlotte County, Florida contact the local county or city waste management department and inquire where electronics can be safely disposed of. Nearly every municipality has taken steps to reduce electronic residue from filling their landfills. And like our county they sell the materials to recyclers.

Now that we have a destination for our old PC there is still one task left to take. As computers take a more prominent place in our daily lives, it becomes a penumbra about how much personal information resides on the hard drive. Take no chances. If we have the recovery disks that either came with the computer or the ones we made right after we unpacked the box, use them to put the computer back to the condition that existed as it emerged from its packaging. Something a bit more critical on the PC? There are software programs such as http://eraser.heidi.ie, which will wipe and write over and over on the drive, making data recovery virtually impossible. If all else fails, and this is by far the most fun, pull the hard drive from the computer and use a hammer, sledge, axe, concrete block or your favorite implement of destruction to render the drive lifeless.

What comes around should go around.

FREECYCLE

I took out the trash today and as I was putting it by the curb, I noticed several items that seemed almost too good to throw out. Yet I didn't have a need for them, didn't want to store them, had no reason to keep them and quite honestly, didn't think they had great monetary value. And yet, it still seemed a shame to just send them to the landfill. Why wasn't there another alternative? As I have alleged before, maybe our computer can help us to eliminate items we don't want, and at the same time, prevent them from filling up our landfills.

It will benefit us to take the time to peruse the Port Charlotte, Florida, FreecycleTM Group. The local **website** is http://groups.yahoo.com/group/port_charlotte_freecycle. When you want to find a new home for something --whether it's a chair, a fax machine, piano, or an old door --You simply send an e-mail offering it to members of the group. Maybe you're looking to acquire something yourself. Simply respond to a member's offer, and you just might get it. After that, it's up to the giver to decide who receives the gift, and to set a pickup time for passing on the treasure.

Freecycle is a worldwide organization of local groups whose members post requests for items they need or items they have that are no longer needed but are still very serviceable. Their motto is "We're changing the world one gift at a time!" The mission statement for the worldwide group is "… to build a worldwide gifting movement that reduces waste, saves precious resources & eases the burden on our landfills while enabling our members to benefit from the strength of a larger community." To find a Freecycle group in your neighborhood, use the Internet to navigate to www.freecycle.org. Once there, type name of your city or town.

It is very important that we understand what The Freecycle Network is and what it isn't. It is NOT a place to just go to and get stuff for nothing. It IS a place to give or receive what you have and don't need or what you need and don't have -- a free cycle of giving which keeps stuff out of landfills.

There is a group of about 662 members in Charlotte County and they follow some eleven basic rules that keep the group on track. Some of the more important rules from their website are:

1) No Chat, No Politics, No Spam, No Money, No Personal Attacks/Rudeness.

Grandma and Grandpa, how come you're so smart?
  Website: A website is a collection of related web pages containing images, videos or text.
  We can purchase airline tickets by surfing to the airlines website on the Internet.
  Websites can be for businesses, personal, clubs and other organizations that want a global reach.
  Wrong: The spider built a beautiful website in the corner of the garage.

2) NO TRADING/BARTERING OR OFFERS TO SELL/BUY, PLEASE. If your e-mail program is set to automatically insert an advertisement or link for your business, please edit it before sending.

3) KEEP IT FREE, LEGAL, & APPROPRIATE FOR ALL AGES - This means, for example, no Alcohol, Tobacco, Firearms or Drugs, legal or otherwise. This is our main rule and it's a pretty easy one at that. No advertising your yard sale, as you're looking for money and that isn't free...

4) RESELLING - If you're responding to an offer with intent for resale, you must disclose this to the gifter prior to pickup. This allows the gifter the option of providing the item to someone who will use it personally, if they so choose. In the end, we'd all like to keep an item out of the landfill and gifting to a reseller meets that criteria. Sometimes we'd prefer to directly help one another. The choice of choosing an individual over a reseller is at the sole discretion of the gifter.

Surf on over to http://freecycle.org/manual/index_faq.htm. There you can find some other suggestions on safety when picking up or leaving a gift. Guidelines for creating online posts when either requesting an item you need or offering an item as a gift to someone else.

All it takes is a few minutes to request a membership in the local group. A short time later an e-mail with your membership approval will arrive with all the details you need to get started. Login to the site, take a few minutes to read the FAQs, and pieces about online etiquette and safety, then start to recycle the Freecycle way. Help yourself, help others, and keep one more item out of the landfills.

Have fun de-cluttering, gifting, and receiving! (Martha, let's clean out that closet!)

DON'T DISCARD, RE-USE!

Many folks have moved on from that old XP machine to shiny new PCs. In the process we may find that our old calculating companion while perhaps slow and lacking the bells and whistles of its replacement is still functioning. It seems a shame to relegate it to the scrap heap. So we ponder what fate should befall it. Some of us just can't let go so we store it in the closet, garage or attic. There are of course charities we can donate them to, grandkids or friends, but it is so hard to let go. Maybe there is a way to keep these dinosaurs working and still contributing to our future?

There is a massive demand for computer processing power by organizations involved in research of all kinds. Cancer research, mathematics, climate prediction, astronomy and many other disciplines require almost endless calculations. The cost of assembling computers with the power needed would be prohibitive. A concept called Distributed Computing allows research projects to take enormous amounts of data and spread it out in little chunks to millions of home computers all over the world. Each computer uses idle **processor** time to crunch data in the hopes that, combined with all the other crunching being done, maybe a cure for cancer will be found or a better understanding of the universe.

The only requirements that we have to meet is to make sure our old computer is running, connected to the Internet and then download a small piece of software from the research project we want to participate with. A list of Distributed Computing projects can be found at boinc.berkeley.edu/projects.php. These projects are known to Berkeley and the descriptions are considered accurate. Another list of private projects can be found at boinc.berkeley.edu/wiki/Project_list. To get started, use the old PC to surf over to these sites, review the projects available, choose one and sign up for the project. Most sites simply need an e-mail address and a password. Next download and install a small program. This program uses the computer when it is idle to process data and send the results back to the Project. What a great way to help advance human knowledge and perhaps solve some of the world's biggest problems.

Grandma and Grandpa, how come you're so smart?
Processor: Part of a computer that performs calculations or other manipulations of data.
A computer's processor is often referred to as the Central Processing Unit or CPU.
Some folks consider the computer's processor to be akin to the human brain.
Wrong: "Sweetheart, please clean out the garage," she said. It took a moment to processor statement.

Another great use for an old computer is to use it as a platform for a home surveillance system. If the PC is connected to the Internet we can even monitor the house, rooms, babysitter or pets from remote locations. If it isn't connected to the Internet we can still use it to record all the activity that took place in a given time frame for review at a latter date. The only things needed besides the PC is one or more webcams and some software to run the camera and transmit or record the images. Here is the best part. If we are looking for just some basic software to run the camera then take a look at this site or do a search on the Internet for free webcam surveillance software.

www.ilovefreesoftware.com/05/windows/5-best-free-webcam-surveillance-software.html.

This page lists five free surveillance camera software packages, each with different capabilities. Not recommending any specific one, read all the reports, specs, and features that go with each one remembering that for FREE you get BASIC. If you need more capability it will cost something depending on what is needed. I did grab one called YAWCAM that took about five minutes to install and I could remotely view the goings on in my office.

Don't dump that old computer just yet.

FREE CREDIT REPORTS

Merriam Webster Dictionary defines FREE as: not united with, attached to, combined with, or mixed with something else. It may be time to review the meaning of the word FREE and add an additional usage something like; FREE as in: smoke and mirrors, con job or look out baby because here it comes. Some things are free, a sunset over Charlotte Harbor, a conversation with a burrowing owl or even an evening stroll during Gallery Walk. It seems that the word free is bandied about with little regard to its meaning.

This morning I received my monthly mortgage statement along with a full color flyer showing a happy couple embracing in magnitudes of joy. I presume their bliss was because they had taken advantage of the offer contained in the flyer. I read the flyer, at any moment expecting waves of ecstasy to wash over me, and was amazed that my mortgage company was going to give me a FREE copy of my credit report. I continued reading and there was the reason it was so important to have good credit and in addition to my FREE credit report, I would receive credit monitoring as well. This way I would know as soon as some nefarious character used my credit and good name for disreputable means. What a nice company they are, and imagine they used to make automobiles.

But wait, what is this? If I take my FREE credit report and the credit monitoring they will only add twelve dollars per month to my mortgage payment. $144 per year for my friends at the mortgage company to watch and tell me when my credit is used by someone else? No, I am not permitted to take just the credit report and forego the credit monitoring. So the question becomes, is the credit report really FREE?

Blood is boiling now. I fire up the computer, open a **browser** and type in the search window, "free credit report." First site up is http://www.ftc.gov/bcp/conline/pubs/credit/freereports.shtm. This is the FTC site that gives us the particulars of a federal law entitling every citizen to one free credit report per year from each of the three major credit reporting companies. Surf over there and then click on the link to annualcreditreport.com. Order a credit report from one company, wait four months and order from the next company and repeat after four more months with the last company. Repeat next year. Beware that while the companies are required by law to provide a free credit report without strings, they are not prevented from

---

Grandma and Grandpa, how come you're so smart?
Browser - A program that accesses and displays files and other data available on the Internet.
Internet Explorer, Chrome, Firefox and Safari are examples of an Internet browser program.
I can open up my browser and surf to the airline site to buy a ticket for my next trip.
Wrong: I often go to the store, not to buy anything but to simply be a browser.

---

trying to entice the purchase of useless credit monitoring services. Yes I said useless.

Let's review what a credit monitoring service does. It will supposedly notify you if anything unusual or suspicious appears on your consumer credit report. Kind of like closing the barn door after the horses have run away. How tough is it for someone to steal your credit information? Apparently not too tough. April 20, 2005 MSNBC: Information giant LexisNexis revealed that hackers stole data on about 310,000 of its customers and Citibank sent nearly 4 million letters to consumers last year after a data backup tape was lost in transit to a credit bureau. C/NET February 18, 2005: ChoicePoint has confirmed that scammers culled the personal information of tens of thousands of Americans in a recent attack on its consumer database. Nov. 02, 2004 NEW YORK (AP) Thousands of Wells Fargo & Co. mortgage and student-loan customers may be at risk for identity theft after four computers were stolen last month.

There is another much more effective method that is permitted in Florida by state statue. Browse over to http://www.consumersunion.org/campaigns/learn_more/003484indiv.html and scroll down to Florida to read about how to put a "Security Freeze" on your credit information. A security freeze lets consumers stop thieves from getting credit in their names. A security freeze locks, or freezes, access to the consumer credit report and credit score. Without this information, a business will not issue new credit to a thief. When the consumer wants to get new credit, he or she uses a PIN (Personal Identification Number) to unlock access to the credit file. Florida gives consumers this important weapon to prevent identity theft. If you have been the victim of identity theft, or are over the age of sixty five, then this service is mandated to be FREE. Otherwise there is a $10 fee to place a security freeze on your credit reports. I wonder why credit monitoring is pushed so hard and security freeze not.

Maybe it's time to go cash only!

FOUND MONEY?

Money, Money. It happened again this week. I woke up from a wild dream that I was the CEO of a major car company and Daffy Duck just walked in and handed me 17 billion dollars. Not only that, but I don't even have to explain what I plan to do with it. The week before I dreamed I was a bank CEO and Bugs Bunny hopped into my office and dropped off a giant sack of cash and yelled, "have fun and let me know if you need more," as he left. An unexpected windfall, or as it is sometimes referred to, found money is always a pleasant surprise. Remember the last time you reached in a pants pocket and pulled out a five spot? It brought a smile to your face.

Think back over the years. Were there insurance policies that faded from memory? Stocks or bonds that got misplaced. Water or utility deposits never collected when our residence changed? Bank accounts and safe deposit box contents left behind? Maybe even some un-cashed checks and wages? Have you considered that our erudite electronic savant may lead us to found money? Is it possible that our digitally demonstrative servant might offer us a way to prospect for treasures unknown? Is it possible some cold hard cash is only a few keystrokes away?

Money, Money. Hundreds of companies claim they will find, for a small fee, lots of money lying around just waiting for us to claim it. However, our government requires lost assets to be turned over to the states. All but nine of the states and even a few Canadian provinces have joined together to facilitate reuniting lost assets with their owners. To augment the states' ability to locate lost property owners, MissingMoney.com, a national database, was established in November 1999 and is the only **database** endorsed by the National Association of Unclaimed Property Administrators (NAUPA). MissingMoney.com enables owners to perform comprehensive searches for lost assets.

X marks the spot. Let's start this treasure hunt with a trip to missingmoney.com. There we will learn that this site is a jumping off place for a search in any state we live or lived in. The database maintained by NAUPA is updated monthly and the searches we perform are, hold on to your hats, FREE. (Free cash for FREE,

Grandma and Grandpa, how come you're so smart?
Database - Electronic filing cabinet of information arranged for easy access or for a specific purpose.
I use a database to keep track of all my friends in order to send them Christmas Cards.
Using a database makes it easy to send out personalized form letters via a mail merge.
Wrong: Ten people camping together is a database.

Martha) Start your search by entering your name. Remember, less is more. If you put in John Q. Public then the search will be for exactly that. But maybe your lost assets were made out to J. Q. Public. That will not show up unless you type it exactly that way. So start with just Public. Now every lost asset for any first name, initial or middle name Public will turn up in the results.

If your name appears with a lost asset it will display the name of the state holding the asset and the company or agency that reported the asset to the state. Click on your name, and it will take you to the state website where the real work begins. Every state has a form to fill out and you must be able to prove you are the person the asset belongs to. Dealing with the states in general can take months nevertheless the outcome may well be worth it. One person I talked to about their experience indicated it took almost nine months to work through the red tape, provide the documentation required and then just waiting for the wheels of government to turn. But, they got a check for twelve hundred dollars from some assets lost in the late 1950's. Another friend reported that he received $400 representing a forgotten utility deposit.

Searching for hidden assets is fun too. (Unless there isn't anything for me.) Still after spending some time searching for yourself, you will be tempted to plug in the name of your brother or sister, mom, dad, acquaintances and so on. My son is on his grandmothers favorite grandson list now because he happened to find her name on the list. He e-mailed her and she got a little cash out of it. Tell your family and friends about this site. Somebody's experts, estimate 1 in every 8 people in the U.S. have missing money.

Money, Money. Maybe dreams can come true.

LOTS OF FREE STUFF

FREE. Say it with me, FREE. There are many things in life that are FREE. We can view a sunset, suck in air to breathe and find many neat programs for our computers. (Martha, FREE stuff for the computer!) Let's see what is out there for our computers, things that actually work, are not just thirty day trials or requiring the purchase of something in order to get FREE stuff. (How does something that is free actually result in less money in my pocket?) Are you familiar with the TV ads for a free credit report if you send them $180 a year? Did I miss the memo on the redefinition of the word free? Here are a few things that really are FREE.

Speaking of FREE credit reports go to www.annualcreditreport.com. Do not go to www.freecreditreport.com. Here is the confusing part. Freecreditreport is not free but the site that doesn't mention free is FREE by law. The site www.annualcreditreport.com will give you one free credit report per year per the three major credit reporting companies, Experian, Equifax and Transunion. These companies will try to entice you with amazing deals along the way towards your free credit report so read every page before clicking on buttons. You can run one free report on each company. Run Experian now, then Equifax in four months and Transunion four months after that. This way you can get three FREE credit reports every year.

Next up on the FREE parade are some photo editing software for the casual user. All of these programs can be downloaded and installed on the computer for how much? That's right FREE. I suggest that you **download** a couple of them, try them out until you find the one that meets your requirements and then don't forget to uninstall the ones that are not going to be used. That way there are no confusing surprises. For clean and simple, download Picasa from Google at picasa.google.com. This is a great program for nascent photographers and even has the ability to take your collection of pictures and burn them to a CD-ROM. (if you have a CD burner)

Adobe offers Photoshop Express Editor from www.photoshop.com/tools click on Online Tools. This is a neat program that is web based (no software on your computer) and allows the uploading of two gigabytes of

Grandma and Grandpa, how come you're so smart?
Download - Transfer data from one computer to another. Usually refers to transfers from a larger "host" system to a smaller "client" system.
Microsoft regularly downloads updates to our computers.
We can download pictures from a camera to our computer in order to send them out in an e-mail.
Wrong: Fido went to the backyard and proceeded to download a stinky present.

photos for storage, photo editing and photo sharing either by e-mail or uploading them to a variety of online sites. For the photo newbie, this is a powerful piece of software and the price is ….. Can you guess?

For those that have a need for a bit more intense photo manipulation, go to www.gimp.org and download GIMP 2.4. This is an open license program and very sophisticated. This is for the more advanced photographer but the price remains FREE.

How about computer backups? Have you done one lately? Are there files on the PC that could not be easily reproduced? Old photos, legal documents or even that best selling manuscript you have been working on for three years. HAVE YOU BACKED UP LATELY? If not, then there are some great sites that offer storage space for (I think you know by now) FREE! Microsoft offers Windows Live SkyDrive, www.skydrive.live.com, where you can upload five gigabytes of online storage for FREE. This is a great way to protect important documents from fire, hurricanes, theft or other disasters by storing it offsite. This site is password protected, easy to use, and you can access your files from any Internet linked computer in the world. If you already have a Hotmail, MSN or Live.com e-mail address just log in and start backing up important files. Otherwise take a few minutes to set up an account and then do a backup. Some other sites that offer a limited amount of free storage are MozyHome, www.mozy.com which offers two gigabytes or Dropbox at www.dropbox.com. Dropbox also has a small piece of software that when downloaded and installed allows you to schedule automatic backups of specified files or directories. If the need for additional storage becomes a factor, these sites offer larger storage capabilities at reasonable pricing. Now there is no excuse for not backing up.

There are bushels of free tools, antivirus, file transfer programs, online word processing and spreadsheet programs available. One of my favorites is OpenOffice.org which is a complete office productivity suite that emulates MS Office. The big difference is that the total financial outlay for OpenOffice.org is nada, zero and zip. Just download from www.openoffice.org, install and start using.

I like FREE don't you?

FREE YOUR E-MAIL ACCOUNT

Have you ever gotten one of those questions that makes you stop and think, "Why DID I do that?" I received just one of those questions this week from faithful reader Henry. "Court, why do you use "Hotmail" instead of the regular service providers? It seems that all the people I know that are in "the know" use Hotmail or Gmail. Can you write about it or e-mail me with an answer? As you can see I use Centurylink.com and pay near $35.00 a month for the service."

First, those of us in "the know" don't use Hotmail or Gmail because of some super secret plot to set us apart from the rest of the world. It really boils down to freedom of choice. Let's take Henry's case where he uses Centurylink to send and receive e-mail. Why does he use Centurylink? Centurylink **DSL** Internet Service offers an e-mail account to anyone that buys their Internet Service. In other words, Henry doesn't pay $35 for e-mail, he pays that amount to be able to access the Internet. As a perk, Centurylink gives him, at no additional charge, one or more e-mail addresses to use.

Why would they do that? Because when Henry starts to use Centurylink's e-mail, he gives out his e-mail address to friends and family and he builds an e-mail address book on the Centurylink website. He can send and receive e-mails, and he can use his address book to create new e-mails every time he has something new to send to friends and family. He probably registers at his online banking site with his Centurylink e-mail address, and he uses it when he buys things online from Amazon or other retail websites. The list of uses for this e-mail address goes on and on.

Henry realizes that if he leaves Centurylink for another Internet Service Provider, Centurylink will close his account and all his e-mails will be gone, his address book gone, all the websites he is registered on, banks, stores etc, will no longer be able to contact him. In fact if his e-mail address is the logon name for those accounts he may not be able to even log on. He will have to redo everything. A very strong incentive for Henry to stay with Centurylink and their Centurylink e-mail. Nothing wrong with Centurylink and Centurylink e-mail but there is

Grandma and Grandpa, how come you're so smart?
DSL - Digital subscriber line: a technology that allows high-speed transmission of text, audio, and video, usually over standard telephone lines; a form of broadband transmission.
My Internet Service Provider provides high speed Internet via DSL over the same line as my telephone.
Using DSL I can surf the Internet and answer the phone at the same time.
Wrong: I stopped at the gas station and accidently put DSL in my gas tank.

some lack of freedom should he want to change providers.

So why do those of us in "the know" use so called FREE e-mail accounts such as Yahoo, Hotmail, or Gmail to name a few? Remember that none of these e-mail providers offer a way to get to the Internet. But if you can get to the Internet, then access to these accounts is universal. For example: I can sit in my office, turn on the computer which immediately uses Comcast to reach the Internet. Once on the Internet, I open a web browser like Internet Explorer and surf to www.hotmail.com. Log in and there are all my e-mail and addresses. Now suppose I go on vacation in New Zealand. I walk into an Internet café, log into hotmail.com and there is all my e-mail and addresses.

But here is the real reason I use Hotmail. Suppose our friends at Comcast really tick me off. Not that they ever would, but just suppose. I switch to any other ISP (Internet Service Provider) like Centurylink or NetZero or perhaps I don't even get a provider but plan to use computers at the library. As soon as I get on the Internet, I go to Hotmail.com and there are all my e-mails and addresses. I don't have to notify anybody of a new e-mail address. FREEdom. (Freedom is power, Martha.)

Another advantage with free accounts is that it cost the same to have one or ten. For example, I use a Yahoo account for family e-mails. I use a hotmail account for business, a Gmail account for some of the special interests I have and even a free AOL account for those sites that require an e-mail address before giving information that I want. That way when they send the spam e-mails I know they will, it goes to the AOL address which I rarely look at and AOL empties the inbox of older e-mails automatically.

If you would also like to be in "the know" group, go to any search engine and type in Free Webmail Providers. This search results will take you to a page that list a large number of providers of free webmail and a brief overview of what each one offers.

Now where are those stamps?

CHANGING E-MAIL PROVIDERS

Ying and Yang. This and that. On the one hand, on the other hand. Two sides to every story. It seems that no matter what we think is correct, someone comes along with an equally persuasive argument for another approach. So it is with our email. I spoke with a client that connected to the Internet with Centurylink DSL and was about to move to Comcast Cable for higher speeds. He asked, "Would he have to switch his email to Comcast or could he keep using EarthLink?" EarthLink cost $30 per year and all his friends had the EarthLink address. What should he do?

It is not necessary to switch to the email offered by the Internet provider. There are advantages and disadvantages to any course of action. This case offers some examples of those issues. Many years ago, this client had an EarthLink dialup service. (Martha, remember the beep, BEEP, bEeBEEEeeeeeee sound it used to make?) EarthLink, like every Internet Service Provider offered one or more email accounts with a subscription to their dial up service as a means to prevent users from leaving their service. The marketing idea was once we had an email address we would not want to change it. Remember when we moved from one house to another? Change of address forms, notifying all our banks, utilities etc of our new address. It was a real pain to work through.

When users began to move to high-speed Internet connections, the dial up companies offered to let us keep our email addresses for some nominal amount per month and a lot of folks continued to pay. Then along came companies offering FREE email accounts. Examples are Hotmail, Live, Yahoo, Gmail, MSN and many more. They offer free email accounts but no access to the Internet. To use their email, we must have a connection to the Internet. It can be a service like Comcast or CenturyLink or even an Internet connection available from many restaurants, our neighbor's wireless routers or the public library. If we can reach the Internet we can get our FREE email. If we use the library or other FREE **hotspot** to connect to the Internet and use a free email service does that mean we save twice as much?

Another advantage to free email not tied to an Internet Service Provider is if we decide to change our

---

Grandma and Grandpa, how come you're so smart?
Hotspot: A site that offers Internet access over a wireless local area network via router connected to an Internet service provider.
Many restaurants and local libraries offer free Internet via a hotspot.
Today many cell phones can act as wireless routers offering a hotspot to a nearby computer.
Wrong: When I saw the 75% off sale at the store I new it was a hotspot to be.

provider because of cost, location or service, we don't have to notify anyone of our change of address. For example, I have had about five different Internet providers over the last fifteen years but my email address is still the same Hotmail.com address it has always been. How difficult is it to change email addresses? What steps should we take before taking the plunge? Here are some suggestions.

First ask, are we comfortable with Webmail or do we prefer a client based email program like the old Outlook Express or the current Window Live Mail, Eudora, Thunderbird etc? If we prefer a mail client then research the FAQ (Frequently Asked Questions) in the help section as to which free email providers also make POP3 (Post Office Protocol) available. If they don't provide POP3 then only Webmail is possible. Webmail simply means that the mail and the ability to view it are based on a connection to the Internet. A mail client means that the client program actually moves the mail from the Internet to our PC and when on the PC it can be read even if we are not connected to the Internet. This was a great feature back when we had to pay for Internet connection time by the minute. Today with always on connections this isn't an issue anymore. Client based mail also poses the possibility that if our computer crashes we could lose all our email and addresses. Webmail, if our computer crashes, just get a new computer, reconnect to the WEB and our e-mails and addresses will be there. Sort of an e-mail backup.

Second, before canceling our old email provider, export our email address book to a CSV file. (Comma separated values) Almost all email providers have this feature available and it makes it very easy to construct a copy of our address book for import to any new email provider we decide on.

Third, from our old e-mail provider, send an e-mail to everyone in the address book. Something along the lines of "Hi, I am switching e-mail provider to XYZ and my new e-mail address is abc@def.com. Please make the change to your address book. If not willing to make this change then it has been nice e-mailing with you."

The reason for sending the e-mail from the old address is that those folks that just hit the forward button to send the same jokes and political propaganda as the 485 other idiots who forward it to us, are too lazy to update their address books and we never receive anything from them again. Great way to cut down junk e-mail.

Changing e-mail providers, easy, fun and if we go with FREE, can provide some FREEdom to change Internet providers as the opportunities arise.

WE LOVE FREEBIES

We love freebies. Admit it. Here the word free and our hearts flutter. We line up at Publix for the free samples of food that employees hand out. Stories of elderly pensioners that used to eat cat food lined up at grocery stores at dinner time grazing on free samples. Golden Corral you have competition. Someone hands us a free bottle of chamois crème and we take it even if we don't ride bicycles or have a gallon of it at home. Third Thursday Gallery walk is successful partly because we can forage for free courtesy of the downtown merchants. Even the world famous Ringling Museum of Art in Sarasota is free on Mondays per a requirement Mr. Ringling made prior to turning it over to the State of Florida. One might argue this freebie is worth $25, the cost of a ticket on any other day, but somehow, all this art and all day to peruse it seems worth a whole lot more.

Did you know that our beasts of **binary** burden can transport lots of freebies right to our fingertips? Our digital domestics can open a floodgate of opportunities for sustenance, service, entertainment and information all for the amazing outlay of zip. So let's fire up our computers, open a browser window to the Internet and find some of the things out there that someone wants us to have for free.

Surf over to www.heyitsfree.net to get started. There are two types of free, the FREE free, and the free if you spend money free, so read each offering carefully. I just signed up for a free bag of Betty Crocker Au Gratin Potatoes. Yes they asked if I wanted to get a regular newsletter from them (I don't) but other than that there didn't seem to be a catch. There was also a modicum of fun involved when they asked for my birth date. I couldn't resist and added fifty years to my age. Next one I'll take fifty years off, which should throw them for a loop. This site is chock full of totally free stuff, semi free stuff and links to other free stuff. Looking for something to do on a rainy day? Spend it in front of the computer and in a few days or weeks your mailbox will be overflowing with gewgaws, munchies and why did I ask for this, stuff.

Don't feel bad about getting something for nothing. Free stuff allows us to determine if a product is right for us before we actually spend money. Additionally, freebies give us a chance to explore new products that we might not have tried. Take a look at some other sites of value, if free is valuable; www.complimentarycrap.com

> **Grandma and Grandpa, how come you're so smart?**
> **Binary** - Base two. A number representation consisting of zeros and ones used by practically all computers.
> Binary systems consist of only two components. Ones and zeros, yes or no, on or off.
> Let's count to three in binary 0, 1, 10, 11.
> Wrong: It's a binary answer, yes, no or maybe.

and www.freestuffheadquarters.com just to name a few of the sites that are available.

Don't forget that Charlotte County also has some free stuff accessible by our computers. If you have a library card, (free) go to charlottecountyfl.com/Library and click on the link for Downloadable Audio Books. This will allow access to over 1100 downloadable audio books - digital versions of the latest best sellers, book club favorites, award winning authors and more that we can download and listen to on our computer or to a wide range of portable devices, including portable music players, portable media centers, Pocket PCs and even select Smartphone devices. We need to download and install free software from the Digital Media Catalog website to play the files.

It took a few minutes to get everything set up, download the software, find my library card, pick a book to listen to and download it to my computer, but now I am listening to a biography of John Paul Jones, founder of the US Navy. All for the amazing price of, say it with me, FREE.

Finally, with all this free stuff, there must be someway to spend some money. But we don't want to squander our hard earned shekels; we want to stretch them till they squeak. Take a look at www.floridacouponnetwork.com, type in your zip code and up pops coupons for saving money on groceries, dining, etc. Select the ones desired, print, spend.

I can still hear coins jingling in my pocket.

EVEN MORE FREE STUFF

I wonder sometimes if anyone has actually looked up the definition of FREE? Dictionary.com defines FREE as: "provided without, or not subject to, a charge or payment: free parking; a free sample." I have no problem with being told that this or that product can be had for a certain price. But nothing sets me off more than being told something is FREE and then discover that my wallet will be a whole lot lighter after I receive my FREE product. Sometimes it can be pretty humorous. A full page advertisement in a magazine boasted that their product was FREE for only $250. Another one I like is "get your FREE credit report for just $180 per year. Is there anything out there that is actually useful and free?

Happy days are here again. While many companies offer free stuff, our friends at Google have put together something they call the Google Pack. This is a suite of programs that can be installed with just a few clicks of the mouse. We can pick and choose the programs we want from a menu of choices. The Pack includes three different Antivirus programs. (Only load one, more is not better but will slow the PC down,) Two different web browsers, Also included is Skype for making computer to computer video calls if we have a **webcam** or just an audio call without the camera. Picasa is included for organizing, editing and sharing our photos and a few other programs that we may find useful. Surf over to pack.google.com to see what is available for your computer. There may be some differences depending on the operating system on your computer. Those computers with Windows 7 seem to have the most choices.

Occasionally I mention a site to download something of interest and someone will e-mail me to tell me the site is wrong or when they click on download it wants them to pay. If after going to the site above, either of these results occurs, then type Google Pack into a search engine to find the site. After that if these two results continue, then there is a reasonable probability that either it has been typed incorrectly or the browser has been redirected by malware.

Google also includes a very extensive help screen should there be problems installing the programs using the Google Updater which is the program downloaded first to our PC and manages the download and

> **Grandma and Grandpa, how come you're so smart?**
> **Webcam** - A digital camera transmitting images to the World Wide Web often in real time.
> I make video calls to my grandkids, using webcams we can see each other and wave to each other.
> Webcams can allow us to have a virtual meeting where we can all see one another at the same time.
> Wrong: Spiders with video cameras are not using a webcams.

installation of the programs we pick. If for some reason the Google Updater cannot be installed, remember that all the programs listed are available for download individually from the respective manufacturers.

Another interesting site to visit is www.av-comparatives.org. This is an organization that evaluates antivirus companies' software each year and tries to pick the leader in protection. This site is very remarkable because of the statistics provided. I have had the misfortune to hear sales folk at certain big box stores state that we should buy their antivirus program because it is better than anything else. Mention that we use Comcast as our Internet Service Provider and receive Norton antivirus at no additional charge (Martha, he didn't say it was FREE.) and they state that Norton isn't any good. This site gives an unbiased report. Interestingly one of their top rated antivirus companies is one of the FREE programs included in the Google Pack.

Free does exist, if only for a little while longer.

SIMPLE MONEY SAVERS

Money; the one thing that always seems in short supply. It seems sometimes we spend it solving a problem only to slap our foreheads at the simplicity of the solution. This week I share experiences from the computer tech world that, had our user spent just a few moments looking at the problem it might have saved the cost of a service call.

The non functioning wireless mouse and or keyboard. Folks purchase a wireless mouse and or keyboard. They eagerly remove the rapper, insert batteries, follow the installation instructions and happily type or mouse away. After a year or so, they discover the mouse doesn't work anymore. They slam it on the desk, unplug it from the PC, talk nice to it, then bad to it and still it doesn't work. Throwing up their hands they call their favorite computer tech. The tech walks in, picks up the mouse, asks for new batteries, pushes the connect button on the wireless transmitter, pushes the connect button on the mouse and in a moment the mouse is working fine. Problem solved. Very expensive batteries.

The non starting PC. Occasionally a PC user will sit down, hit the power button on the desktop and nothing, zip, nada. No lights, no fans, not even a hard drive spinning up. Frustration engulfs. The call goes out to those wonder people, the computer tech. The tech arrives, tries the power button. Silence reigns but the tech is nonplussed. First, checking to see if the **surge protector** strip is turned on, and then making sure both ends of the power cable are inserted firmly into the PC and the surge protector. Still no joy. Next we plug the power cable directly to the wall socket and more often than not, the PC powers up. Now we move the plug to a different socket in the surge protector. If the PC lights up then the socket in the surge protector was the culprit. Problem solved, no money saved.

The Invalid Trust Certificate message. Trying to login into a secured website like our banks, insurance companies or e-mail providers we occasionally get a message telling us that the Trust Certificate is invalid or language to that effect. The Trust Certificate allows our computers to talk to the banks through a secure encrypted format. Part of that encryption is based on the date of our computer and theirs. The dates and times cannot be more than a few minutes off. The Invalid Trust Certificate message means that the date on one of

> **Grandma and Grandpa, how come you're so smart?**
> **Surge protector** - A device designed to protect electronic devices from transient power surges.
> Florida is the lightning capitol of the U.S. so a surge protector is imperative.
> Some surge protectors can also protect cable and phone lines from power spikes.
> Wrong: I built a new seawall to be my surge protector.

the computers is way off. Before calling in a tech, check the time and date of the PC and if necessary change to the correct time. Problem solved. Money saved.

The PC starting then shutting off. A call to the local tech. The tech presses the power button and the PC starts and runs and runs. Shutting the computer down the tech starts it over and over, each time the PC remains running until ordered to shut down. Nothing seems amiss. The tech asks the user to start the PC so that each step taken is observed. The user presses the power button holding it in until they see activity appearing on the screen. Then the digital domestique shuts down. The tech explains that holding the power button in more than six seconds activates the computer's mercy kill. It is used when a PC will not shut down. Press the button once, release and the computer happily starts up. Problem solved, lesson learned.

Ben Franklin said it best, "A penny saved, is a penny earned."

EVEN MORE MONEY SAVERS

Do we love to save money? We clip coupons, watch for sales, even frequent garage sales. A woman told me her fall clothing needs for three daughters was purchased at yard sales for a few dollars. Maybe we can save a few bucks with our computers too.

Computers need an active, up to date **antivirus** software package to protect us from infection. Buy a new computer and the salesperson will pitch the need for and purchase price of, the antivirus program de jour. But many of us use broadband providers for our Internet service. In Charlotte County that is primarily cable (Comcast) and DSL (Centurylink). One of these providers includes a full antivirus suite in the cost of the Internet subscription. Comcast provides Norton Internet Security. These programs do not automatically appear when we sign up with these companies, the user must go to the Comcast homepage and sign in (you will need your username and password) to download and install the package. This is a full antivirus suite and not some watered down package. There is no advantage to buying it versus downloading from the ISP.

There are perhaps a few folks in Charlotte County still using dial up connections for their Internet access, some are using satellite, mobile Wi-Fi or connected through a Wi-Fi provider that does not offer an antivirus package with the subscription. Not to worry, there are many very effective **antivirus** programs available for free. (Martha free is a beautiful thing.) Just a few to whet the appetite are Microsoft Security Essentials, (www.microsoft.com/security/pc-security/mse.aspx, AVG Free Edition, AntiVir Personal Edition Classic, and AVAST 4 Home Edition. Surf over to www.download.com and search for the Free version of each of these programs. Use caution when downloading these programs. With the exception of the Microsoft product these companies also have a paid version and try very hard to convince the user to pay for the upgraded version.

It's nice to save money and do something good for the environment. The day came when I needed to move on from my old, but faithful Windows XP machine to a shiny new Windows 7 PC. The local waste management department can direct us to a drop off location for electronics. Staples also provides a recycling program for non working electronics, details can be found at this site,

> **Grandma and Grandpa, how come you're so smart?**
> **Antivirus:** Programs to detect and remove computer viruses.
> Occasionally, I personally check to make sure my antivirus software is up to date.
> To prevent a virus from infecting my computer I installed a leading antivirus program.
> Wrong: An antivirus program requires a prescription from the doctor.

www.staples.com/sbd/content/about/soul/recycling.html.

We can also use our computer to save money in other areas as well. Fire up the computer and surf over to autos.msn.com/everyday/GasStationsBeta.aspx to track the lowest price gasoline available in our area. Type in a zip code and a very extensive list of gas stations appears with the price of gas displayed. There is even a map that will display where the station is and we can get driving directions to it.

Still another site to visit is www.groupon.com. At this site coupons are offered for sale that reduces the cost of dinner or other products such as movies etc. An example was a theatre show that was offing $30 tickets for just $15. Just purchase the ticket, print the coupon and present it at the box office.

I hear extra coins jingling in my pocket.

PRINTING ON THE CHEAP

How is the transition to a paperless society coming along at your house? Sure, we bank online, pay our bills online, even have our monthly statements emailed to us. Our friends and family email instead of write an actual letter and catalogs from our favorite stores arrive in our email box. Even our local newspaper has an online edition. It must be true because printers have reached new lows in pricing. A basic color printer can be had on sale for under $40 and a combination scanner, fax, copier and printer can be found on sale for under $100. But, if no one is printing why is the price of printer ink so high?

Many folks try the discount ink cartridge sellers with varying degrees of success. Some of us use Walgreens and other stores that refill our ink cartridges for lesser amounts of money. Do these methods work? They might. Printer manufacturers tell us using a non genuine cartridge will void the warranty. If our printers are out of warranty what difference does it make? To get us past the purchase of a printer, manufacturers include ink cartridges with every new printer. But look on the pack and it will say these are starter cartridges and do not contain a full load of ink. So it isn't long after setting up a new printer that we need to head to the store for new cartridges. It can get expensive. We can measure our ink cost by taking the number of sheets we print and dividing it into the cost of the ink we buy. This is called "**cost per page**."

Cost of supply is only half the equation. If we can reduce our printing, or if we must print, reduce the amount of ink used we can extend the life of each cartridge and consequently reduce our "cost per page." How can we reduce the amount of ink used? Certainly if we are printing a picture of our favorite grandchild on high quality photo paper there is nothing we can do. We want the best picture our money can print. On the other hand, printing emails, letters or news items off the web require only that we can read them. There are a few tricks we can use that not only reduce the amount of ink used but also lessen the time required to print a page.

Printers generally have three print settings. Fast Draft, Normal and Best. Different manufactures may give them different names and may even include further obfuscation by adding Fast Normal and Economy and

> **Grandma and Grandpa, how come you're so smart?**
> **Cost per page:** Price of the ink cartridge divided by the cartridge's page yield.
> Use the Internet to find the page yield and then calculate the cost per page of a new printer.
> A cheap printer can actually be very expensive if the yield or cost per page to print is very high.
> Wrong: Congress never calculates the cost per page they hire for each representative's office.

Maximum. What do these names really mean? They refer to the number of dots per inch or DPI. The more dots per inch mean more RAM memory is required to create the print job, more ink is laid down per inch and the printer seems to take forever to print a page. As a rule of thumb, Draft mode uses 300 dpi, Normal mode 600 dpi and Best or Photo mode uses 1200 dpi. It is easy to see that if we print everything that doesn't need high quality in Draft mode we will use far less ink and our cartridges will last longer and our wallet will thank us. (Martha, I want my wallet to thank me.)

We can squeeze even more out of our ink cartridges. Since black ink cartridges for most printers are much cheaper than color cartridges, we can set our printers to print with only the black ink. Now we have a printer set to print in draft mode, 300 dpi, and use only the black print cartridge. Our cost per page just went down a little more.

Let's get started. There are two places we can set the draft mode and black ink only conditions. One is at each print job and the other is to set the printer defaults to draft and black ink only. If we print mostly text and items that do not require high quality, consider setting the printer defaults. This means that every time we print the printer will use draft mode and black ink only. Click on Start – Control Panel – Printers and locate the icon for the printer. Right mouse click on the printer, and then select from the menu Printer Preferences. There under Quality will be the option to use Draft mode. Then look for a tab labeled Color and put a check mark in Print in Grayscale and Black Ink Only. Changing these items here will lock them into the printer so every print job after that will print with these conditions. However, should we want to print a picture in full color with Best dpi levels we can change the print preferences from the print dialogue box that appears before each print job.

Maybe our wallet will thank us too.

I'LL DO IT MYSELF

This is the tale of a fateful day. The computer wouldn't start. Don't need a computer tech; I can fix it by myself. I'll just call the computer company and they will tell me what to do. One ringy dingy, two ringy dingy... hello, what did you say? "Yes Susie, I will be great pleasure to solve computer problem. I am standing here beside myself with fix and oh by the way my name is Rashid, no I mean Mark and I love American Baseball."

Mark, my computer will not start. "I am sorry to hear that Susie, and I will satisfy you with correct action. May I please know the error message you are getting?" **Error message**? Wait, I will try to start the PC again. There it is, it says KRST system failure please call your manufacturer. "Yes, that is common problem, please remove all cables from the computer and hold in power button for sixty seconds." Rashid, I can't get one cable loose. It is a big cable with blue on the end and two pointy things at either side of the end.

"Yes, that is the monitor cable and the pointy things are the screw nuts that hold the end tight to the PC. Please turn them counter clockwise Susie and the end will come loose from the computer."

How about that Mark, it came loose. I held the button in for sixty seconds. Now what? "Please reattach all the cables and try to restart the computer." Same message Rashid. Next? "Susie, please remove the power cord, and then the side panel of the tower." How does the side panel come loose? "Press the release on the back of the tower and remove the side panel." Rashid, we seem to have reached an impasse. I cannot get the side off. I am going to get my next door neighbor who knows about this stuff to come over and help me. "That is a very good idea, Susie." (sound of doors opening and closing)

Mark, Rhonda is here and neither of us can get the panel off. We are pulling, lifting, hitting, pushing and it won't budge. Maybe we should get George from across the street, he has a computer. Rhonda says it is ridiculous that two people can't remove a side panel; it would be absurd if three people can't get it off. Wait a minute, it just popped off. Rhonda, what did you do? "I smacked it and it must have gotten the message."

> **Grandma and Grandpa, how come you're so smart?**
> **Error Message:** Message indicating that an incorrect instruction has been given to the computer.
> To trouble shoot computer problems it is helpful to record all error messages.
> The error message indicated that the problem was in the program installation.
> Wrong: Robin Hood would use his long bow to send instructions to his merry band by error message.

Ok, Mark what next? "Susie, there is a battery there that looks about the size of a ten Rupee, so sorry, a quarter. Carefully remove it." Rhonda, I can't get this out can you? Rashid how does the battery come out? "Susie, there is a small clip that holds the battery in. Push it gently and the battery will pop out." Rhonda, was that the battery that just flew across the room? "No, that was my second fingernail." Maybe we should get George. "Never Susie, we got this far we can figure it out. Oops, that was the battery. It just jumped out by itself." "Susie, take battery to store and purchase same battery, then call me when you have it installed."

Mark, we have the battery installed now. "Very good Susie, now put the side back on and reattach all the cables and start the computer." Rashid, we have an impasse, we cannot not get the side to go on. Rhonda should we get George now? "NEVER!" "Susie, we do not need the side on to see if the battery will solve the problem. Please try restart computer." Success Mark, the computer is running, but the side is off. I can't put the computer in its place until I get the side back on. "Susie, I cannot tell you how to put side on; you will have to call the case manufacturer for specifications on panel putting on. Thank you Susie for calling, goodbye."

Rhonda, where are you going? How do I get this side on? (sound of door slamming, feet running) I guess I'll call my favorite local computer tech.

Hi Susie, what's the problem? Can't get the side on? Ok, it goes on just like this. Anything else? Battery was bad? Happens occasionally, I carry spares with me. Use something small and pointed to move the clip and the battery pops right out. No, I never have broken a fingernail getting one out.

Sometimes, it pays to do it yourself. Or not.

COMMON COMPUTER LINGO

So I said to the auto mechanic, "It's making this squeaking grinding noise when I go around corners. I think it is probably something to do with the steering wheel." The car comes back all fixed and the repair order says that the ball joints and tie rod were replaced. Two completely different sentences that both meant the same thing needed to be fixed. The computer world is very similar. There is a lingo that technicians use and there is a language the rest of us use. In an effort to bridge the communications gap here are some common terms, their translation (what they mean) and how to use them in a sentence.

Let's start with **Operating System**. The operating system or OS as it is referred to, is the most important program on a computer. A computer must have an operating system to run other programs. Operating systems perform basic tasks, such as recognizing input from the keyboard and mouse, sending graphics to the monitor, keeping track of files and folders on the hard disk, and controlling attached devices such as disk drives, scanners and printers. It makes sure that different programs and users running at the same time do not interfere with each other. Common Operating Systems in use are the Windows programs, XP (2001-2006), Vista (2007-2009), and Windows 7 currently the system sold on new machines. There are many other systems used on different computers and for different requirements. UNIX, Linux, AmigaDos and MAC OS X, are all tasked with making the computer work. If wondering what OS is running on a PC, click on the Start button – Programs – Accessories – System Tools – System Information. There we will find the OS currently in use on our machine. Or watch the computer as it starts up. There will be a screen that tells us the OS installed. Let's use this term in a sentence. My computer uses the Windows 7 Operating System.

Next up on the term list is URL. URL stands for Universal Resource Locater. This is the address of files and web pages located on the Internet. When we type http://www.someplace.com in the address bar of our browser, a page opens up in the browser window with information from that location. Think of it as a house address. Our address may be 123 Anystreet, Port Charlotte, Florida, USA. Anyone anywhere in the world sending a letter to that address would know that it would arrive here in our mail box because that is where we are. The URL is the same, but uses a different format including colons, forward slashes and periods instead of

Grandma and Grandpa, how come you're so smart?
Operating System: The essential program in a computer that maintains disk files, runs applications, and handles devices such as the mouse and printer.
The operating system that is the focus of Grumbles from the Keyboard is Windows, either XP, Vista or 7.
It is imperative that we keep our operating system patched and updated.
Wrong: When gambling, one must have an operating system to consistently beat the house.

commas and spaces. The http:// part of the address is called a protocol identifier and it indicates what protocol to use. Http stands for hypertext transfer protocol which is used to transfer web pages from the Internet to our web browser. FTP:// refers to file transfer protocol which is used to transfer files from the Internet to our computers or vice versa.

The previous paragraph referred to a browser, short for Web browser, a program used to locate and display Web pages. The two most popular browsers are Microsoft Internet Explorer and Firefox. Coming up strong behind them are Chrome and Safari. All of these are graphical browsers, which mean they can display graphics (pictures) as well as text. Think of a browser as a television. Instead of having fifty, hundred or even 500 channels, the browser has millions and millions of channels each one reached by changing the URL. (Martha, I know that one.) Browsers can even display video and sound available on the Internet. For example, surf over to Pandora.com and build a "radio station" of just the music styles preferred. The browser will display the URL, and then play the music selected.

Want to buy some airline tickets? Open any browser window and type the URL for Travelocity, an airline or cruise line in the address bar.

There are literally thousands of terms specific to computers. If one of them makes us stumble, type it into a search field, let the search engine find the URL for a page that defines the term and add it to our vocabulary.

Who said an old dog can't learn new tricks?

WHAT EVERY PC USER SHOULD KNOW

When does a computer repair person progress from the New Delhi based ex-pizza delivery person/tech support agent to the wizened old veteran computer tech? I don't know either but with more than sixteen years tackling computer problems there are a small number of common threads that weave their way through the calls for help. Here are a few things every computer user should know.

Record error messages. Error messages contain clues, if not outright explanations, why a program or computer crashed. Giving a tech the contents of the error message might save hours of trying to recreate the error and time is money. If necessary, write the message down verbatim, take a picture of it with a camera, use Snipping Tool (Vista and Windows 7) or a screen print if necessary but capture the information. Feeling adventurous? Plug the error message into a favorite search engine like Bing, Yahoo or Google and see if others have had the problem and perhaps found a solution.

Know when to single click or double click. Double clicks open windows. Double click an icon on the desktop to start a program. Single clicks are for opening links on a webpage, buttons in **dialogue boxes**, highlighting a picture or selecting from a menu. To make everything a single click if desired, open the Control Panel and single click on Folder Options. When the dialogue box opens select the radio button labeled Single Click to Open an Item. Now a single click will start programs. If we double click by mistake we may open the program twice or crash it if it can't be run multiple times simultaneously.

Make finding things in the Control Panel easier. By default the Control Panel displays icons in Category view. This is pretty and organized but makes finding specific Control Panel items time consuming if not difficult. Open the Control Panel and click Classic View on the left in Vista and use the dropdown in Windows 7 to select large icons. This makes following instructions that refer to a specific Control Panel function much quicker.

Know which operating system (OS) is running on the PC. A client recently told me she had tried one of the topics in a column and couldn't get it to work. She would get so far and then she couldn't find the next step in the process. Following up, the column clearly stated that the process was available for Vista and Windows 7. The client was running Windows XP which didn't have the capability to perform the function. Many problem

> **Grandma and Grandpa, how come you're so smart?**
> **Dialogue Box:** Displayed on a screen that conveys information, or requires a response from the user.
> Click print and a dialogue box opens that allows us to select number of copies or print quality.
> The dialogue box popped up requesting permission to install a new program.
> Wrong: At Easter some folks dialogue box instead of an egg.

solving solutions are OS specific. A solution for a Windows 7 problem may not work when applied to Windows Vista or XP. One way to determine the operating system is to find My Computer (XP) or Computer (Vista and Win 7) right click on the icon then choose Properties from the menu. In the window that opens will be listed the operating system running on the PC. Rule of thumb, computers purchased prior to 2007 will be Windows XP, prior to 2010 will be Vista and machines purchased after that will be Windows 7.

Drag and drop windows is a handy way to move open windows around on the desktop. At the top of any window there is a border called the title bar, for most of us it is blue but depending on the desktop theme it could be any color. Use the mouse to left click anywhere in that box and hold the mouse button down. While holding the button down move the mouse and the cursor will appear to drag the window anywhere we want it to go. When we have it positioned as desired release the mouse button and the window will occupy its chosen location.

Many users believe only one window or program can be open at a time. A few years ago that may have been prudent from a resources perspective, but today with Vista and Windows 7 we can open and utilize multiple windows, programs and tasks at the same time. For example; open a word processing program and move it to the right side of the screen by dragging it as far right as it will go. In Vista and Windows 7 the word processor will occupy one half of the screen. Let's pretend we are working on a report and need some supporting statistics. Open our favorite Web browser and drag it to the left of the screen and it will pop into the left half of the screen. Now we can find our information on the Internet and type it into our report as we go. Want some soothing music while working? Click the Start Button, type media player or ITunes in the search field and play our favorite music while we toil. Open a bookkeeping program to check the finances, run an antivirus scan and search for that lost file. Our digital domestique can do it all and all at the same time.

But with multiple programs and windows open how can we move easily from window to window? Next time our calculating companion is multitasking, hold down the ALT key and tap the TAB key. This keyboard shortcut has been around since Windows 3.0 and until Vista was referred to as Task Switcher. Vista and Window 7 kept the functionality but renamed it Flip. Users may press Alt - Tab to switch to any running program. The list of tasks is kept in order with most recently used tasks listed first. Running programs also deposit a program icon on the desktop toolbar which can be clicked on to restore a program to full screen.

Sometimes we just want the desktop. With numerous programs open it can be a chore to find the minimize button on each screen as we work our way back to the desktop. For a quick leap back to the desktop use the Windows Logo Key and the D key simultaneously. All open windows will immediately be minimized (not shut down) and the desktop available.

While we're at the desktop, are the icons scattered all willy-nilly across the screen? Would it be easier if they were in some semblance of order? Find a blank area of the desktop and right mouse click. A context menu will open and on the menu will be a choice labeled View. Click on View and a submenu opens with some interesting choices. One is auto arrange which will line up all the icons starting on the left of the desktop and moving right. We can also sort the icons by name, size or type. We also have the choice of making the icons larger or smaller. If we are an ordered person select align icons to grid and the desktop icons will line up like perfect soldiers. A little more relaxed? Remove the check mark from align icons to grid and grab each icon with the mouse and drag it to that special place we have in mind.

Sometimes we wish to print just a piece of an article from the Internet. To accomplish this instead of printing the entire webpage, highlight the section we wish to print, then click File – Print. When the print dialogue box opens look for the section labeled Page Range and click on the radio button labeled Selection. Click print and only the highlighted section of the webpage will print.

Another basic function that saves time is the double click on a word in a document or webpage. Many times I watch as a user carefully and slowly drags the mouse over a word to highlight it so it can be copied or cut from a text document. A much faster way is to double click on the word we wish to cut or copy and the word is automatically highlighted for us. As a bonus, if we triple click a word in a webpage the entire paragraph will be highlighted.

Trying to read an article on the web but the type is just too small? Text on any Webpage can be quickly enlarged. With Windows XP, Vista or Windows 7, press Ctrl and the plus or minus keys (for larger or smaller text)

If our mouse has a scroll wheel on it we can also enlarge the entire Web page or a text document by pressing the Control key as we turn the wheel on top of the mouse.

When reading a long webpage article an easy and quick way to scroll down is the tap the space bar on the keyboard. This will scroll the webpage one full screen at a time. Hold down the shift key and tap the Space bar to scroll back up. If however our hand is on the mouse, look over at the scroll bar on the right side of the webpage. We can click on the rectangle in the scroll bar and drag it up or down; we can click on the up ▲ or down ▼ arrows at the top and bottom of the scroll bar which will move the screen one line at a time. Click in the scroll bar below or above the rectangle and the page moves one full screen up or down.

Occasionally we need to fill out a form on line. Perhaps setting up a new account, typing in a first name then another field for the last name, address fields, city, state and so on. To save time we can press the Tab key on the keyboard to move from field to field rather than taking our hands off the keyboard to grab the mouse, move the cursor to the next field, clicking the mouse and then putting our hands back on the keyboard to fill in the field. Hold the shift key down to move backward through the fields.

Sometimes, and no one ever seems to figure out how they managed it, we get a window that opens very small. Or we have multiple windows open and they are on top of each other. Almost all of us know that if we click on the center small box in the top right corner of any window we can enlarge it to full size or return it to the original size we opened it in. We can also adjust the size and position of any window on the computer. Drag the top strip of any window to move it. Move the cursor to any edge or corner of an open window, look for the cursor to change from the arrow to a double headed arrow ↔ and then drag the lower-right corner or edge to resize it.

Windows knows that sometimes we make mistakes. For example, when we delete a file from our computer the unwanted file goes into the Trash or the Recycle Bin. It isn't actually deleted. We still have the opportunity to open the Recycle Bin and restore the deleted item to its original place. That is also why if we try to free up space on our hard drive by deleting documents and pictures nothing changes. It's like collecting all the waste baskets in the house and putting them in the barrel in the garage. We haven't actually removed the trash from our property until the trash is taken away by the city. On our computers we need to empty the Recycle bin to actually remove the files from our computer. The recycle bin is usually on our desktop and if we right mouse click on it we can choose Empty Recycle Bin to complete the deletion of unwanted files from our computer.

Don't forget the CTRL key and Shift key when trying to select multiple files. For example, many folks ask if there is a faster way to delete files from the documents folder rather than highlight a file, click delete, answer the confirmation and then move on to the next file. To select a list of items, click on the first item in the list and then hold down the Shift key on the keyboard, move to the last item in the list and click on it. Now all the files between the first one and the last one selected are highlighted and we can delete, move or copy the selected files. The CTRL key allows us to randomly select files for action. We need to highlight the first file we want by clicking on it once then hold down the CTRL key and move through the display of files clicking on the ones we want to include with the first one selected.

Windows also includes context menus. These menus are specific to the application or window that is specified. For example; if we right mouse click on the desktop, a context menu appears with a list of options that we can perform on that window such as New Folder, Personalize etc. On a webpage if we right mouse click a context menu appears that actions from Print to search among other choices. Remember, right click means "What do you want to do?" Left click means "Do this."

Probably the most important basic piece of information every user should know is that hard drives fail. Murphy's Law says that a hard drive will fail immediately upon downloading irreplaceable pictures or completion of the most important document of our lives. Consequently it is imperative that we have a backup of any thing we can't afford to lose or recreate. How to back up those items? There are many methods to choose from and they will be discussed elsewhere in Grumbles From The Keyboard.

It only gets easier. School's out!

MORE STUFF EVERY USER SHOULD KNOW

"Do you mind if I watch?" I hear this simple phrase over and over when I sit down at a sick computer and prepare to perform PC triage. I actually enjoy having an audience when I work and encourage my clients to ask any question they wish. Sometimes the question requires a very technical answer to be specific, but I can usually translate the answer into layman's terms so the concept can be grasped. Let's journey through a typical computer house call and see if some of the terms that pop up can be demystified.

"Why are you hitting that key?" the client asks. I am trying to start the computer in **SAFE MODE** by repeatedly tapping the F8 key immediately after seeing the computer manufacturer's logo screen. What is SAFE MODE? Safe mode starts the computer but loads as few programs as possible and only those **devices** necessary to display information and accept input. IE: the mouse, keyboard and video so we can see the screen. Think of it as turning off the burners on the stove before trying to clean it. Safe mode just makes it simpler to find problems.

"I tried the F2 key but didn't know what to do after that." Pressing the F2 key (some computers use the ESC key or the F10 key) opens up the BIOS setup. BIOS stands for Basic Input/Output System. This is a little set of instructions built into the BIOS chip on the system board that tells the computer how to start. It tells the computer to look for a hard drive and operating system, a floppy drive, CD drive, mouse, keyboard and a video output interface. Here we can make modifications in what the computer looks for first, whether or not we want it to require a password before loading the operating system etc. We can also turn on or off integrated (built into the motherboard) components that we need or don't need. For example, say we added a super duper monster video card to the system for all the games we play. We would go into the BIOS and turn off the integrated video card so the new card would be the one the computer uses.

"Every time I try to go to a website I get the 'Page cannot be displayed' message." When we try to see something on the Internet we use a Web Browser. A Web Browser is the software used for viewing pages on the web. Two examples are Microsoft Internet Explorer and Mozilla Firefox. Internet Explorer is the Web Browser that is included with the Microsoft operating systems, Windows XP, Vista or Windows 7. Third party

---

Grandma and Grandpa, how come you're so smart?
Safe Mode: A diagnostic mode of a computer operating system.
Boot a PC into Safe Mode by, repeatedly tapping the F8 key when the manufacturer's logo appears.
I use Safe Mode to diagnose rogue software problems on my PC.
Wrong: Use a long match to light the grill in safe mode.

companies add little pieces of additional software to Internet Explorer called Add-Ins. Occasionally one of these Add-Ins interferes with the smooth operation of Internet Explorer and causes problems such as 'Page cannot be displayed.' We have the option of removing all the Add-Ins one at a time to try to find the guilty party, but sometimes it is faster just to reset the browser back to its default settings. To do this, go to Start - Control Panel - Internet Options. Click on the tab labeled Advanced and down near the bottom is a button labeled Reset. Click it and the browser is return to its original state. Any needed Add-Ins will then reinstall when they are required.

Blank Stare. This usually occurs when I ask a computer user if they backed up all their DATA. Technicians bandy about this term as if everyone should know what we mean. Data is simply anything that we created and added to the computer's storage system. This can be pictures, music, letters, greeting cards, spreadsheets or forms. Everything else that is considered programs, (the software that does things) usually doesn't get backed up because we should have the original disk that we used to install the software. It is easy to reinstall a program but if that letter to the editor wasn't backed up it is gone forever.

Finally, the computer world does have some humor associated with it. I wanted to share this definition of a printer because it seems to be right on target. Printer: A printer consists of three main parts: the case, the jammed paper tray and the blinking red light.

What would you like to know?

CREATE SHORTCUTS TO SAVE TIME

Sometimes the simplest things bring the most pleasure. Working with our calculating assistant often gives pause as we wonder why there isn't a simpler or quicker way to get from here to there. Our computers really want to make life easier for us; they just aren't sure what it is we want them to do. Perhaps there are a few small things we can do that will enhance the harmonious dance between man and machine.

We are all familiar with icons that appear on our desktops after installing some new piece of software that allows us to open a program with a couple quick clicks of the mouse. Much preferred to clicking on the Start button then Programs then scrolling looking for the program folder then opening the folder in order to reveal the icon for the program we want to use and then clicking on the icon to start the program. But, what about the programs already on the PC for which there are no shortcuts to the desktop?

Let's imagine that we use the calculator regularly. To place a shortcut on the desktop for a particular program such as the calculator, click on Start - Programs - Accessories. In the list of programs under Accessories, find the icon for the Calculator. Use the right mouse button to click on the icon. A context menu will appear and from that menu click on Send to: and from the sub menu choose **Desktop** (create shortcut). A new icon appears on the desktop that allows us to double click and open the calculator directly. The same process can be used to create a shortcut for our favorite games or any other program loaded on the PC.

If we have a website that we frequent, perhaps a bank or a favorite shopping site we can add a shortcut to the desktop that will allow us to go directly to the site rather than using favorites or typing the site address in the URL bar every time we need to visit that site.

Find a blank spot on the desktop and right mouse click on the desktop. A context menu appears with choices for us to make. Click on the word New and from the submenu select shortcut. A dialogue box appears asking us to type the location of the item. Type in the web address of the site we want the shortcut to take us

Grandma and Grandpa, how come you're so smart?
Desktop: A display on a computer screen comprising background and icons representing equipment, programs, and files.
The desktop on my computer is the jumping off place for everything I do.
Many folks put a picture of their favorite item as the background to the computer's desktop.
Wrong: It was difficult to put a pen and pencil on the computer desktop and make it stay.

to. For example: www.sunnewspapers.net. Click next and give the site a name and click Finish. A shortcut appears on the desktop which opens a browser window and loads the site directly.

Another technique for adding a shortcut to the desktop for a website is to surf to the site and then anywhere on the webpage (but not on a picture) right mouse click to open a context menu for that page. From the context menu select create shortcut. A message will appear asking if you want to put a shortcut for this website on the desktop. Click yes and a new icon appears on the computer that will take us directly to the site.

Sometimes we just want to be everywhere all at once. Internet Explorer, Firefox and Chrome allow us to create multiple homepages. A home page is the very first website we see when we open a browser window. Example: Open Internet Explorer, click on tools, Internet Options. In the dialogue box that appears under the General tab we see a box labeled Home Page. Here we can enter several websites click apply and the next time we open Internet Explorer we will see multiple tabs, one for each site we specified. Click on a tab and move quickly between sites. My browser has six home pages which allow me to check different e-mail accounts, news sites etc.

It is a simple thing.

E-MAIL NETIQUETTE

If there is one button in any e-mail program that should be removed, I would vote for the forward button. This one button is responsible for more heartache, hard feelings, misunderstandings and general mayhem than any other feature in an e-mail program. How can that be? We all forward things to other people. Notification of upcoming meetings, family messages that need to go to Aunt Jane or pictures of the new grandchild. These are all good uses of the forward button. One might argue that forwarding jokes or declarations of our political orientation is a necessary expression of love for our fellow man. As the recipient of untold e-mails, neither requested nor solicited, I make liberal use of the delete button and simply consider them to be one of those things accepted because they cannot be changed.

There is one type of e-mail forward however that is just plain rude. This is the e-mail that contains all the other addresses in the senders address book and sometimes the e-mails of all the folks in the address book of the person that originally sent the e-mail. There can sometimes be hundreds of peoples' e-mail addresses in the top of an e-mail. Why is this rude?

Let's start with a simple question. Did the sender of the e-mail receive permission from all the people in the address book to distribute their e-mail address to everyone else? Did the sender get clearance from all these folks to allow the inevitable deluge of return e-mails they are bound to get? Did the sender really care who received these e-mails, or were they just too lazy to organize the address book into those who have to know, and those who don't really care? Why didn't they use the **BCC** (blind carbon copy) function?

There is nothing wrong with sending forwards. There is a bad way as described above and there is a good way. Let's take a look at some ways of sending forwards that will lower the disgust of those inundated with hundreds of e-mail addresses of people we do not know.

The first thing we do when we receive a must forward joke or political commentary, (Martha, it was on the Internet so it must be true.) is hit the forward button. The moment of decision has been reached. Many people

---

Grandma and Grandpa, how come you're so smart?
BCC: A way to send an email message without revealing the recipient's address.
When sending e-mail to multiple recipients, I always use BCC to hide other addresses from each individual.
BCC stands for Blind Carbon Copy.
Wrong: The fisherman returned home with a BCC. (Big Catch of Cod)

at this point have created a group that contains all the folks they forward e-mails to. This is an acceptable tool as it saves us the effort of typing in all the e-mails of the folks we want to receive the e-mail. However, many people click on the "To:" field and enter the group or e-mail addresses here. This ensures that everyone that receives the e-mail will be able to see the e-mail addresses of every person that receives the e-mail. There is a very simple way to solve this dilemma. Instead of using the "To:" field, click on the "BCC:" field. BCC stands for BLIND carbon copy. Enter the group or e-mail addresses into the BCC: field and the recipients will not be able to see the other 200 e-mail addresses we sent to. But we are not done yet.

After hitting the forward button, (or the reply button) the e-mail becomes fully editable. In other words we can change anything in the body of the e-mail. Or put another way, we can remove all the e-mail addresses in the body of the e-mail that the previous sender wasn't competent to remove. To remove all the e-mail addresses in the body of the e-mail, use the mouse to highlight all the e-mail addresses. Position the cursor by clicking the left mouse button in front of the first e-mail address and then, holding the left mouse button down, drag the mouse over all the remaining e-mail addresses. Now use the delete key on the keyboard to remove permanently all the e-mail addresses.

Once we have sanitized the e-mail by removing or hiding all the e-mail addresses we can hit the send button and deluge our friends with our prolific font of critical information.

If however they continue to send e-mails unwashed. Don't get upset, just have fun. Hit the Reply All button and send every e-mail address revealed a newsletter or advertisement and put in the body of the e-mail that this communication is courtesy of; and put in the original senders name. I have discovered that it takes only one Reply All and either I receive cleaned up e-mails, or none at all from that sender. Either way works.

Forward this column to everyone in your e-mail address book. Or at least those that don't clean up their e-mails. They may get the point.

SIMPLE MAINTENANCE ITEMS

It has been a long week. First, install new exterior mirrors, rear view mirror and a new antenna on the car. Then choosing a paint to use on the bathroom walls because some law requires that the bathroom paint be changed every few years. (At least that's what I'm told.) On the upside however, I can see the cars around me clearer and the bathroom will look better. So maintenance is a good thing. A pain to be sure, but worth the effort.

When it comes to our computer, maintenance is also a good thing. There are four maintenance items that should be on a to-do regularly list. These items improve performance, keep it running at top speed and protect our privacy. So where to start?

Let's start by freeing up some disk space. Click Start, point to All Programs, point to Accessories, point to System Tools, and then click Disk Cleanup. The best part of this utility is that it identifies which files can be safely deleted and lets the user decide whether to delete some or all of the files to be removed. Clear the check boxes for files that we don't want to delete, and then click OK. When prompted to confirm that we want to delete the specified files, click Yes.

As a rule, **temporary Internet files**, consume the largest amount of space because the browser saves each webpage visited so it can be accessed faster the next time the page is visited. To limit the amount of space temporary Internet files can use, click on Start, Control Panel, Internet Options, then on the General tab. There is a section called Temporary Internet Files, click on Settings. Under Disk Space to Use set the amount of disk space allocated to Temporary Internet Files. There will be a recommendation from Windows there but feel free to experiment with high or lower numbers.

Next we want to speed up the computers ability to access files. Over time, your computer writes files in pieces where ever there is space on the hard drive. In computereze this is referred to as Fragmentation.

Grandma and Grandpa, how come you're so smart?
Temporary Internet Files: Website data cached on a computer's hard drive to facilitate loading the page on the next visit to the page.
Temporary Internet files on the computer can be used to determine where we have been browsing.
Downloaded programs or pictures will be stored in the Temporary Internet files unless directed otherwise.
Wrong: Temporary Internet Files cannot be cached at the bank.

(Martha, he's making some moonshine.) This slows down the computer's ability to open files because it has to look for and find all the parts and piece and put it back together again. There is a Windows utility called Disk Defragmenter that checks all the files and folders. The utility moves fragments around so each file and folder occupies a single space on the disk. Each file is stored end-to-end without fragmentation so that reading and writing to the disk speeds up.

Again, Click Start, point to All Programs, point to Accessories, point to System Tools, and then click Disk Defragmenter. When the dialog box opens select the drive that is to be defragmented and first click on the button that says Analyze. Always analyze first because it will tell you if you need to defragment. It can take several hours to complete a defragmentation so if it isn't necessary don't do it. One of the questions I am asked is: "How often should I defragment my hard drive?" This is what Microsoft recommends. Run Disk Defragmenter if you add a large number of files, free disk space nears fifteen percent or new programs. I would suggest you at least run the Analyze test once every two or three months just to check the condition of the drive. For Vista and Windows 7 users, Defragmentation is built into the operating system, occurs on a regular schedule and other processes are not affected because defragmentation runs as a low priority process so you don't have to worry about it. To alter the schedule for Defragmentation, go to Start – Accessories – System Tools – Disk Defragmenter and make any changes required to the scheduled run times.

Like any machine, a hard drive can develop errors or bad areas (sectors) on the disk itself. Bad sectors will slow down the hard disk. To check the integrity of the files on the hard disk we want to run the Error Checking utility. This utility scans the drive for bad sectors and looks for file system errors to see whether specific files or folders are misplaced. Make sure that you close all open files before running this utility. Click on Start and then on My Computer. In the My Computer window, right-click the hard disk you want to search for bad sectors and then click on Properties. In the Properties dialog box, click on the Tools tab. Click the Check Now button. In the Check Disk dialog box, select the Scan for and attempt recovery of bad sectors check box, and then click Start. If bad sectors are found, choose to fix them.

Always check to make sure to have an up to date anti virus program (Comcast users can get one form their ISP for no additional charge) and a spyware program, (Microsoft provides Windows Defender to XP users for free and it is built into VISTA and Windows 7.) Additionally there are a multitude of free anti-virus programs such as Microsoft Security Essentials. The free programs generally stick to the basic functions, antivirus, firewall, anti malware etc. The paid versions generally have lots of extra features some of which may be useful, some are duplicates of windows functions and other are just interesting or annoying.

One more thing to check is the number of programs running when you start your computer up. Press the CTRL, ALT and DEL keys on the computer simultaneously to bring up the Windows Task Manager. Click on the Processes tab and look at all the programs running. If you recognized some that are not used, go to Add and Remove Programs (XP), Programs and Features (VISTA and Windows 7) and uninstall them.

Everything listed above except the anti virus programs came with the Windows operating system and won't cost a dime.

Got to go, the paint doesn't seem to be putting itself on the bathroom walls.

DELETING HIDDEN FILES

An interesting email arrived this week and it intrigued me enough to share it with you. Faithful reader Jodi writes, "I have approximately 100 files listed in my Windows File Folder. They are all highlighted in blue - Most begin with $NtUninstallKB followed by six non sequential numbers and ending with $. I've been told I can delete them, but I want to make sure I'm not deleting something that will affect my computer. I have plenty of memory, but just knowing they are there annoys me. What the heck are they?"

The short answer is, these files represent the uninstall mechanism for all the Windows updates that get installed either manually or automatically on any computer running Windows as the operating system. If we click on Start - Control Panel – Add and Remove Programs (XP) or Programs and Features (Vista and Windows 7) and put a check in the box that says show updates or with Vista, Start Windows Updates – Show History we can see all the updates that are loaded on our computer. If we are having performance issues and there is some hint that one of the updates are causing the problem we can highlight it and then click on remove to uninstall the offending update. When we click on remove, it actually links to the uninstall mechanism mentioned in Jodi's email and that feature removes the update.

What intrigued me with Jodi's letter is that the files mentioned are normally not visible. In fact there are thousands of files and folders on the computer that by **default** (the nominal condition) are hidden from the user's view. There are specific steps that need to be taken in order to see all these hidden files and the average computer user has neither the knowledge nor reason to view these files, much less consider deleting them. They are hidden because they are important or critical to the functioning of the computer.

But, just like telling a kid not to go out of the yard which simply ensures that the first chance he gets, he is gone like the wind, I am going to explain how to make the invisible visible and how to really mess up a computer. (Martha, remember the cookie jar?) Click on Start – Control Panel – Folder Options. I find it easier to maneuver around if I have the control panel set to Classic view in XP or Small/Large Icons in Vista and Windows 7. A window will open with three tabs along the top. Click on the tab labeled View. In the box labeled Advanced Settings, about eleven lines down is a line that says Show Hidden Files and Folders, click on

> **Grandma and Grandpa, how come you're so smart?**
> **Default:** A value or setting that a device or program automatically selects if no substitute is specified.
> I changed the installation folder destination from the default location to a new folder.
> When setting up Windows, Internet Explorer is the default browser.
> Wrong: Yes I knocked over the lamp, default is mine.

the radio button to display all the hidden items. Now as we navigate around the files and folders on the computer we will see many files and folders that are a little lighter in color or blue and hadn't appeared before.

Most of these hidden files should never be touched. If you decide to delete them, or rename them or do anything to them at all, there is a very high probability that your computer may not work or won't work well. However, the files that Jodi refers to can actually be deleted without affecting the operation of the computer. Be aware though that if you delete the uninstall mechanism for the Windows Updates; you will not be able to uninstall the updates if they should prove to be problematic. Now some of my more adventurous readers will immediately delete these files, then go to Start - Control Panel – Add and Remove Programs, highlight one of the updates, click on remove and an error message will appear that reads the item cannot be removed it may already have been removed would you like to delete the entry. Click yes and the update disappears from the list. Trust me, the update is not gone, but the link to it is.

Can you delete hidden files? Yes you can. Should you delete hidden files? Probably not, unless you know what they are and how they will affect the system after they are gone. My rule, leave them alone, they are hidden for a reason.

Please don't pull on Superman's Cape.

RESOLVING DUPLICATE E-MAIL CONTACTS

Sometimes technology actually addresses one of the issues that have bugged me for years. Surfing the web this week, I came across some techniques and new **software** that was actually useful in my daily routine. One of the things that I dread is working through my address book looking for duplicate and or incorrect entries. For example, I have an email contact that used to be abc@earthlink.net, but now they are abc@embarqmail.com. Both addresses are in my email address book but only one of them is correct. If I had only a few email addresses in my address book, it would not be an issue to manually find and edit/delete duplicate entries. But if there are hundreds of addresses….what a nightmare. Worse yet, what if there are multiple address books with duplicate entries?

I use multiple email accounts. Hotmail Live, Yahoo, Comcast, Gmail and even Aim are domains that I use for email. All except Comcast are FREE. I use one for sites that have information I want but they require that you give them a valid email address. I know that the reason for the email address is that they are going to send me junk mail on a historic scale. So, I give them one of the email addresses I never check. Spam away! But the others all have specific functions. One is business, one is family, and the last research related. Several of the email accounts have large address books with the attendant duplicate entries. Cleaning up duplicate entries was a major job until recently.

Let's review some of the methods we can use to address duplicate email entries. If you have a Hotmail Live account, and 280 million folks do, Microsoft feels your pain. Hotmail Live will now add new addresses for existing contacts to the same contacts entry, rather than create new contacts as it did in the past. And there's a new wizard that will help you remove duplicate contacts. Open Hotmail and then click on the Contacts. In the upper right corner click on Options, then click on Clean Up Duplicate Contacts. Hotmail will identify entries that have duplicate items in them, list them, allow you to edit, merge or delete them and preview the new entry before we save it making it a permanent change.

> **Grandma and Grandpa, how come you're so smart?**
> **Software:** Programs and applications that can be run on a computer system.
> In order to play the Mahjong game it was necessary to load the software onto the computer.
> My Webcam is hardware but the program running it is the software.
> Wrong: After wearing the same clothes for a week they no longer felt like software.

Yahoo Mail does a similar function. Sign into your Yahoo! Contacts and click Tools in the Contacts header bar. Then click Clean up Duplicates on the right side. The tool automatically searches for possible duplicate entries in your Yahoo! Address Book and displays them in a list. Next to each contact, the tool indicates the number of entries that are potential duplicates, as well as the type of duplicate: exact or similar. Double-click any name or ID in the list to review the person's info. On the right, under "Merge Preview", you'll see what a merged entry for this contact would look like. What do you think—do you like it? If so, click Save and Next.

Gmail has a very similar function, sign in to Gmail, open Contacts and click on the More Actions button. From the menu choose Find and Merge Duplicates. Gmail will locate all the duplicate or similar contacts and display them for us. We can then decide to merge the information or make alterations if they in fact should be separate.

At this time AIM does not have a handy wizard for finding and merging or deleting duplicates but I am sure they will in the future. But what about Outlook Express? How do we handle duplicates there? This is not as simple as the duplicate wizards of Yahoo and Hotmail but not impossible to do. Open Outlook Express, and then open the address book. Above the list of contacts, there are some header labels such as Name, Email Address, etc. If you click on the header labeled email address, it will sort all the listings by email address and we can see duplicates listed one after another, allowing us to select and delete the duplicate entries. We can also click on the header labeled Name and the program will sort by name, showing us duplicate entries for a specific person with different email addresses. Select and delete the duplicate, or if it is a different email address, add the email address to the first entry and then delete the second entry.

Those using Microsoft Outlook have built into Outlook 2010 something called Duplicate Contact Detected which notifies the user if they try to enter a contact that already exist. If this happens Outlook will present the user with two possible choices. Either we can make a slight change to the duplicate entry so that it will enter as a new contact or we can allow Outlook to merge the two contacts into one.

Neat and orderly, that's the way I like it.

WHERE'S THE MANUAL?

"You are what you were when," said Dr. Morris Massey. The values and thought processes we use everyday are rooted in the experiences that shaped them as we grew up. After decades of use these values and thought processes become ingrained and automatic. We judge the world around us by the world we knew as we matured. Sometimes it is very difficult to make the leap to the current unless someone points out the steps required to do so or provides a manual. This does not preclude our learning new steps; we just can't make the association between new ways of doing things and how to accomplish the same results we are familiar with.

One of the more common complaints I receive is, "my computer didn't come with a manual." I remember manuals. Thick, sometimes bigger than the product itself, indexed, table of contents, appendix, asterisks, pictures, Fig.1-4, and bedizened with colored tabs to separate sections. Those were the good old days. I would spend hours reading the manual after attempting to operate the new item but before actually being able to get it to work. I know some of us still have a box full of manuals for the appliances we bought in 1973, the four cameras we owned and don't have anymore and of course the manuals for lots of items that are still in the house we sold in 1999. (Martha, where's the manual for the 1982 Sunbeam toaster?)

Why don't items have manuals anymore? Are new items so good that we can simply turn them on and they will anticipate our every whim? Anyone that has tried to install a printer knows that plugging it in is the easy part. How to operate it poses the problem. Yes, we know that printing and shipping paper is a big expense. But even if an item arrives without a hard heavy manual, do not despair. The manual, in a virtual way, does exist. It is at your fingertips.

I was recently given a very sophisticated bicycle computer that a friend had replaced. It was light years ahead of my old one so I decided to install it and configure it for my bicycle. Lots of buttons, display screens, wires, sensors and other unidentifiable items, but no manual. I'm old enough that my first thought was where is the manual? However, I also know that the total sum of human knowledge is contained on the Internet and available with a few keystrokes. I sat down at my computer and typed the name and model of the bicycle computer into my favorite **search engine**. It doesn't matter which one, Google, Yahoo, Bing or any one we

Grandma and Grandpa, how come you're so smart?
Search Engine: A program that searches documents for specified keywords and returns a list of the documents where the keywords were found.
There are many search engines available such as Google, Bing, and Yahoo.
Simply type into a search engine the question or topic and little spiders roam the web to find the answer.
Wrong: Looking for a parking space at the grocery store does not make my car a search engine.

prefer. Immediately up came the manufacturer's website with links to all kinds of products, how-to's and other extraneous information. Not having the time to peruse through everything I revised my search to the model number and the word manual. The search results took me directly to the manual for the computer. I printed off only the specific pages I needed and successfully installed the device.

Several things in this example are of note. There are manuals for everything. They are just not printed and shipped any longer. The advantages are; cost of course, but also if there is a mistake in a manual or a new procedure needs to be incorporated, the manufacturer can update the manual immediately and only the current and correct one is available. Another bonus to online manuals is the ability to print only the pages that pertain to our situation. My bicycle manual was twenty one pages long but I needed only the four pages on installation. I can always go back and get other pages if needed. Convenience is another plus. How many hours have been lost looking for a manual we know we had, but just can't lay our hands on? The online manual is always a few keystrokes away.

Finally, online manuals benefit from new search technology. The search for a model and manual took me directly to the manual. But search engines today are very understanding when it comes to finding things. Talk to them just like we do when asking friends for information. Want to know how to get a sum for a column of numbers in a spreadsheet? Go to a search engine and type the question as if you were talking to the computer. "How do I add a column of numbers in Excel? The search engine will go out and find all the websites that demonstrate the process. Some will have tutorials, pictures etc, but one of them will explain it in a fashion that makes sense. No table of contents, appendix, glossary etc. Just straight to the answer.

You will be what you are then....

WHERE'S THE "HOW TO?"

How to? How often do we ask that question? How to paint a house, how to have a green thumb and of course how to work my computer? Clients purchase a new computer and complain that there is no manual on how to use it. Folks ask, "is there a class I can take or a book I can buy that will tell me how to…" The immediate answer to that question is no. There is no one book or class that can cover everything. However, do not despair. There are solutions to these questions and for the most part they can be low or no cost.

Keep in mind that a computer connected to the **Internet** is a repository of all knowledge in the world. The question's answer does exist "out there." The hardest part is figuring out how to ask the question and then sift through the answers to find one that solves the problem. For the answer to any question, start with a search engine. There's a question. What is a search engine? A search engine is a program that searches documents for specified keywords and returns a list of the documents where the keywords were found. A search engine sends out a spider to fetch as many documents as possible. Another program, called an indexer, then reads these documents and creates an index based on the words contained in each document. It attempts to provide the searcher, us, with the documents that it feels are significant to our search. The results displayed are ranked with the most likely answer to your question at the top of the list and those with decreasing likelihood follow. Note that since many search engines make money from advertisers that pay per click, their listings may favor an advertiser ahead of the one that actually contains the answer you need. Some examples of search engines are, Google, Yahoo, Live Search, Ask, Yahoo, Bing and many more.

Remember when searching for an answer, to go to the source if possible. Example: We use Outlook Express, Outlook or Windows Mail to receive our email from Comcast. However, every time we take our laptop on a trip the emails just won't come in or go out. We could type in a search engine, Comcast mail while traveling and we might get the answer. It makes more sense however to go to the Comcast webpage, click on help and then search only the Comcast Help section for the answer. There we will find a step by step procedure for reconfiguring our mail program to send and receive mail out on the road. Problem solved.

Be specific when asking a question. Typing in, "How do I work my computer," will get millions of

Grandma and Grandpa, how come you're so smart?
Internet: A global system of interconnected computer networks serving billions of users worldwide.
We can use the Internet to pay bills, send e-mail and search for information.
Teach a person to use the Internet and they won't bother you for weeks.
Wrong: Al Gore invented the Internet.

responses but unlikely the one we want. Ask, "How do I add a column of numbers in Excel," and many step by step tutorials, with eight by ten glossy pictures will appear to help solve the problem.

Let's take a common question I hear all the time and see if we can answer it. If the solution here isn't to your liking, use a search engine to look it up. How do I cut, copy and paste? The function of cut, copy and paste will allow you to easily copy or move data between one application and another or copy and move files and directories from one location to another. It wasn't too many years ago, a person would carefully use an Exacta knife to cut out sections of a newspaper or magazine, stick them on a clipboard, carry them over to another document, slap some glue on them and place them in the new document where they needed to be. Or once the clippings were delivered to the person with the new document, that clerk would vigilantly copy them word for word into the proper paragraph. We accomplish the same thing electronically with our computers. Use the mouse to highlight the words or paragraph we want to move, click on edit to see a menu then click on Cut or Copy. Now go to the new document or email and place the cursor where we want the copied item to be and click on edit again to see the menu and now the choice Paste is available. Click on Paste and our document now receives the Cut or Copied section.

How many answers can you find? Look them up.

FIND ANSWERS WITH A SEARCH ENGINE

As most of us do from time to time, I misplaced my sunglasses the other day. I could not remember the last time I wore them, nor where I might have laid them down. Looking out the front door, I could see by the intensity of the sunlight that I was definitely going to need them. (Yes, I have a spare but I couldn't find them either.) First place to check was the car. Why I did that I don't know because it is a scientifically proven fact that what ever you are looking for will be in the last place you look, not the first. (This is a universal law, not a theory.) If only we could figure out what the last place was, it would save hours of fruitless searching. As you already know, no sunglasses in the car.

I stood there trying to think of where they might have been and wishing I could simply Google it. Wait a minute maybe I could **Google** it. Not literally of course, but why couldn't I apply the same principles to my search that Google does when someone attempts to search the World Wide Web for a specific topic? For the unwashed out there, Google is an Internet search engine. It contains an index to perhaps ninety percent of the all the Web sites in the world. There are others, Yahoo, Alta Vista, Bing to name a few, but I happen to like Google and it seems others do as well. How do I know that? More and more I overhear people say, "I'll Google that and see ….." I have yet to hear anyone say, "Let me Bing that a minute." So off to my virtual Google search I go to see if I can find my sunglasses.

First thing to do is to pick a topic to search. The topic for me was Sunglasses. So I type sunglasses in my mental Google and trillions of hits come back as to where a pair of sunglasses might be found. There are sunglasses in the house, in other peoples houses, in cars, stores etc. So that search was pretty meaningless simply because it was far too wide-ranging. I needed to narrow the field down by setting parameters on my search. Next I tried sunglasses and my home address. Google automatically puts the word "and" between the search terms and so this search limited my results to possible places to look in my house. (now we are getting somewhere) But this is still too broad a search field. The key to finding specific items is to narrow the search as much as possible.

> **Grandma and Grandpa, how come you're so smart?**
> **Google:** Google Web Search is a web search engine owned by Google Inc.
> Google received several hundred million search requests every day.
> Google is just one of many search engines available to us such as Yahoo, Bing, and Excite etc.
> Wrong: When I first met my wife I was all Google eyed over her.

To limit the field even more, I used the minus sign. Google recognizes the minus sign as indicating an excluded item. So, in my case I typed in, sunglasses address –bathrooms, since I had used the facilities earlier and hadn't seen the sunglasses in the bathroom. So now I had narrowed the search down to the rooms in my house that were not bathrooms. (getting closer) Next I wanted to reduce my search to an even tighter range. I typed in sunglasses address –bathrooms +countertops. Google sees the + sign as a required search string even though it may be considered extraneous (every house has countertops) and normally might not look for that term. The results told me there were only two countertops in my house. Victory was near!

I was so confident, that before I went to look, I actually sat at my computer and went to www.google.com and this time typed in "Happy Days" using quotation marks before and after. Google then considers the words between the quote marks as a complete phase and looks for results with that exact phrase in it. This search brought up the lyrics to the song, exactly what I was looking for. Singing the words to "Happy Days", it took me only a minute to search both of the countertops in the house. Sure enough, no sunglasses to be found.

What's the moral of the story? Sometimes you just can't get what you want.

ONE MINUTE FIXES

English Novelist, Aldus Huxley said, "Speed provides the one genuinely modern pleasure. So fasten your seatbelts, hang on to your hats. We are going to look at quick, simple one minute fixes for a variety of common computer problems. Raise your hand when you are ready.

Problem: One day we open Internet Explorer to surf the web and all the icons, menu headings (File, Edit, View, Favorites etc. are gone, vanished into thin air. What will we do? Reach up and tap the F11 key on the keyboard. This keystroke toggles the Internet Explorer window from Full Screen, (no menus, icons etc) to normal mode where all our favorite tools can be easily accessed.

Problem: We boot up our computer and when the desktop becomes visible there are no **icons** on it. Not a single Shortcut to our favorite program, not even the Recycle Bin. What will we do? XP and Vista are slightly different. With XP pick any area on the desktop and click the right mouse button. This will open a menu. From the menu use the left mouse button to click on Arrange Icons By. A menu appears and on it will be Show Desktop Icons without a check mark beside it. Left mouse click on Show Desktop Icons to put a check mark beside it and all the icons on the desktop will reappear. Like the look of a clean desktop? Repeat the steps to remove the check mark and all the shortcuts are gone. Not gone, just hidden. Folks using Vista should Right-click the desktop, point to View, and then click Show Desktop Icons to make all the icons to reappear.

Problem: We find an article on the web that we want a hard copy of. We click on the printer icon in the toolbar or click on File, Print and out pops the article on the printer. Wait a minute; the print is so small we can read it only with a magnifying glass. What will we do? Two factors to consider. The width of the paper in our printer is 8.5 inches. A webpage is much wider than that. If we simply click print, the computer tries to make the entire webpage fit on an 8.5 by 11 inch piece of paper by shrinking it down until it fits. Consequently the text is squashed like an armadillo on US 41. But not to fear, webpage creators know that we really want to print only the article or email not the entire page. So somewhere on the page, and sometimes it is obvious but others may take some looking for, there will be a button that says Print or Printer Friendly. Remember this button is

Grandma and Grandpa, how come you're so smart?
Icons: A computer icon is a picture on a computer screen used to navigate a computer system.
Over the years the computer desktop became covered with icons.
Icons make it easy to open and close programs and files when using my computer.
Wrong: When asked if he could perform the task required, he answered icon.

on the page, not up in the toolbar. Pressing this button causes the webpage to print only the article or email in 8.5 by 11 inch format instead of the entire page. Now the text will be normal size and we can put away the cheater glasses.

Problem: Sometimes we experience error messages with Windows or some of its various components, Windows Media Player, Internet Explorer, Office, Outlook Express just to name a few. Problems during installation or uninstalling can be time consuming and frustration. What will we do? Surf over to support.microsoft.com/fixit. Microsoft provides a multitude of Fixit modules for automatically resolving many of the most common problems. The Fixits are segregated by product so if we have a problem with Internet Explorer, just click on Internet Explorer from the navigation bar and look for the Fixit description that most matches the error message or problem. Click on the one that addresses the issue, a page opens describing the problem, the actions the Fixit will take and there at the bottom is a button that says, "Fix this Problem." Microsoft will then make changes to our computer that will resolve the predicament.

Problem: Tiring of constantly clicking on Start – All Programs then looking for that program we use all the time so we can click on the icon so the program will open just to use it for a while. Wouldn't it be nice if there was a shortcut on the Desktop that we could simply double click to open the program? What will we do? For the last time, Start – All Programs, then find the program we want a shortcut for. This time however, right mouse click on the program. A menu appears. Click on Send To. A sub menu appears and we want to click on Desktop (Create Shortcut). Now we have a shortcut to our favorite program on the Desktop we can access directly.

Just call me Speedy.

RESOLUTIONS FOR A NEW YEAR

The New Year is here. That special first day has arrived and with it the time honored tradition of making resolutions which we would like to do, might try to keep but most likely the year will end and we will be able to recycle those same resolutions for the next year. Let's see if there are some resolutions that pertain to our faithful electronic savants that we just might keep. Since the successful completion of these resolutions correlates directly to how soon we start them, let's initiate a few of them right this instant. Grab a cup of coffee, take a seat in front of our digital domestique and let's exercise a resolution or two.

Resolve to keep the computer clean. Grab a flashlight or turn up the lights and examine the case that surrounds the PC. Whether it is a desktop tower or a sleek laptop, we will find vents that allow air to flow through and help cool the hardworking parts and pieces inside. Chances are good that these vents are filled with dust, dog or cat hair or other foreign debris. This detritus can cause overheating which shortens the life of our computer. If working on a tower, remove the side of the box and look inside the box. Often this inspection reveals fans and heat sinks filled or clogged with dust. Use a can of compressed air to blow all the dust out of the vents, fans, heat sinks and the fan located in the tower's power supply, identified by the power plug leading from it to the power strip.

Is the screen is covered with dust, fingerprints, paw prints or other visually distracting goo, use a soft cloth, (eye glass cleaning cloths for example) and some eyeglass cleaner or similar gentle solution to lightly wipe the screen clean.

Resolve to protect our computing companions. Power strips or surge protectors can be the difference between a new computer and just a routine Florida power outage. How old is the one on the floor protecting our calculating concubine? Every time the surge protector does its' job, it gets weaker until it is no more effective stopping a surge than the outlet on the wall. If the strip is more than a few years old, purchase a new strip. It's very cheap insurance. While shopping for surge strips, consider a **UPS**. (**Uninterruptible Power**

Grandma and Grandpa, how come you're so smart?
UPS: (**Uninterruptible Power Supply**) A power supply that includes a battery to maintain power in the event of a power outage for a limited time.
Fortunately my UPS prevented the loss of the letter I was writing when the power went out.
The equipment plugged into the UPS should be the PC, monitor, modem and router at a minimum.
Wrong: When the power went out I waited a long time for the UPS truck to bring some more.

Supply) These devices not only have surge protection, but they also have a battery backup which will prevent our computer from crashing in the event of a power outage and give us a few minutes to shut down our beloved binary buddy gracefully.

Resolve to stay up to date. Next up on the New Year list should be to ensure that recommended updates are installed. Click on the Start Button, then right mouse click on My Computer (XP) or Computer (Vista and Windows 7). This will open a menu. Click on Properties. In the window that opens up the operating system will be listed. Windows XP should display Service Pack 3; Vista should present Service Pack 2 and Windows 7 will list Service Pack 1 as of the middle of 2011. Now click on Start and then Windows Update. The system will connect to the Internet and search for missing updates for the Windows Operating System. Install any updates that it finds listed as Important or Recommended. Other important updates that should be installed are for Java, Adobe Flash, Adobe Reader, and Adobe Shockwave. Read carefully the agreements for installing these updates. There is often a check box already filled in that says some toolbar or other piece of parasitic software will be installed as well. Remove the checkmark to prevent mysterious things from magically appearing on the screen.

Three resolutions made and kept. It's going to be a good year.

UPDATES: TAKE'EM OR LEAVE'EM

Consider the puppy. When the little fur ball first graces our doorstep, it runs around, barks, chews, sleeps and other things that aren't quite as cute. As each day goes by, our puppy changes, feet get bigger, weight goes up, the bark deepens and it begins to learn some instructions. We **update** our training, dietary supplies, bigger bed, and more trips outside. Pretty soon the puppy is fetching the paper each morning, guarding the house when we are gone and fulfilling the role of dog. Even now we update eating schedules, toys and outdoor trips just to keep our canine companion at its peak physical condition. The point is we update our environment each and every day. Nothing stays the same. If we fail to update, things don't work the way they should or we expect them to.

Our calculating companion is very much like the puppy. We bring it home in a box, set it up and connect it to the Internet. Almost immediately it will reach out and grab updates to help it perform its proper role. How often do we see a little window in the bottom right corner of the screen that announces there are updates available? How do we know which updates are necessary, which we can live without and which ones we should decline?

Why should we install updates at all? Updates serve several purposes. Some simply provide additional information that allows a program to perform its function. Anti virus programs can't do their job if they don't know what viruses are out there. Consequently, these programs receive regular updates from their company's servers that give them instructions for detecting and removing new viruses. Other updates can fix problems that are found after the release of a product. Much like an automobile recall except that we don't have to bring the software to a dealer. Updates are downloaded to the software and usually automatically installed. Some updates add features and functions, the accounting software Quicken is an example. Quicken downloads updates to tax tables, bank connections etc, that allow users to input data into the software without having to type everything by hand.

Which updates should we install? Updates from Microsoft for their operating systems are very important.

> **Grandma and Grandpa, how come you're so smart?**
> **Updates:** A relatively minor release or version upgrade to an existing software product that adds minor features or corrects bugs.
> Major software companies recognize that things that worked today may not tomorrow, hence updates.
> Most updates are downloaded automatically from the Internet and installed as specified.
> Wrong: Going out to dinner with a person taller than ourselves might be considered an update.

Updates from MS often close security holes that have been found, patch idiosyncrasies that people have complained about or streamline the way the operating system runs. Windows has built in an automatic update system (Windows Updates) that checks for and installs new updates from MS. It requires little attention from us. Microsoft also makes available to computer manufactures the ability to update hardware drivers. Hardware drivers tell computers how to run things like the mouse, keyboard, disk drives, video etc. These driver updates are not usually downloaded and installed automatically but are made available within the Windows Update module. To check if there are any driver updates for you computer, Click Start and then Windows Update. Windows updates are labeled important or critical and third party driver updates are usually labeled optional.

The rule of thumb on optional driver updates is; if you aren't having any problems then the updates are not necessary. But if experiencing some problem, for example your monitor seems to flicker, look for a video driver update and install it by clicking on the listed update in the windows update.

Other updates that we see regularly and should install are for Java, Adobe, Flash and Shockwave. These programs enhance web content and while not critical, allow our web browsers to display the latest web content written to take advantage of new features and capabilities. Other updates occur infrequently and may or may not be important. Our printer manufacture will offer updates. They notify us of an available update and tell us what it is and allow us to install it or not. HP is diligent in sending many updates for their printers and computers. However, read the descriptions of the updates carefully because some of the "updates" are sales shills for ink cartridges or photo paper.

We sometimes see updates that are installed on our PCs by opening Add and Remove Programs (Windows XP) or Programs and Features. (Windows Vista & 7) While we can see them there, it is generally unwise to remove any unless specifically instructed to by the provider. However, two programs that have regular updates that don't require old updates to be in place are Java and Adobe Reader. The newest version of Java as of this date is Java (Version 6 Update 29). If we have any previous version still on the machine we can uninstall them. This simply makes a bit more room on the hard drive. The current version of Adobe is X. If Adobe 6, 7 or 8 or 9 is still on the PC it too can be removed.

The more things change the more they stay the same.

GET OFF THE UPDATE MERRY-GO-ROUND

Sometimes things just don't work. One problem that seems to come up frequently is a Window's update that will not install. Our calculating companion reminds us that an update is ready to install, the install fails and round and round we go. To see the updates that have failed, click on Windows Updates. If still running Windows XP a webpage will open and click on "Review your update history." A list of updates installed and their status will be displayed. If running Vista or Windows 7 click on the Start button and then open Windows Updates. Click on View Update History to see the same list of installed or failed updates.

From this list we can identify the unsuccessful update install by name. Sometimes these names can be quite long as they describe the update and the systems it applies to. The part of the name we need to know is the KB number. Microsoft labels every update with a KB and then usually seven numbers, for example KB2533501. The KB stands for Knowledge Base and the number identifies the update. So what can we do if an update won't install automatically?

We could simply ignore it. Who needs it anyway? Is it really necessary? Updates are additions to software that can help prevent or fix problems, improve how your computer works, or enhance your computing experience.

There can be a multitude of issues that preclude an update from installing properly, files in use, programs running, spyware or viruses or even a previous install attempt that didn't go quite right. We need to address each of these issues before we try to reinstall the recalcitrant update. Start by opening up Add/Remove Programs (XP) or Programs and Features. (Vista/Windows 7) Click on View Installed Updates to examine all the windows updates currently installed. Search the list for the KB number causing the problem. If it is there, highlight it and click on **uninstall**. Once the problem child is removed restart the computer. If it isn't there close all open programs and proceed to the next step.

Open a browser window and surf to www.microsoft.com. From the menu on the Microsoft site click on Downloads then from the dropdown menu choose Download Center. In the search field on the page type in

Grandma and Grandpa, how come you're so smart?
Uninstall: To remove (a software program) from a computer or computer system.
Deleting program folders does not remove the program but the uninstall provided with the software does.
Programs and Features (Vista and Win 7) or Add and Remove (XP) is where we find program uninstalls.
Wrong: Throwing the computer out the window is not the correct way to uninstall it.

the KB number of the obstinate update. The search will return a page where we can download the update to our desktop. Updates do not take effect until they are installed, but to install updates, you must first download them to your computer. There may be some security pop ups that require our permission to continue depending on the settings we have in place but the goal is to download the update to our desktop. Occasionally there will be several files listed for download. If running XP look for one ending with X86, Vista and Windows 7 usually end with X64. X64 represents 64 bit systems and X86 represent 32 bit systems. (Martha, 86 = 32? I'm so confused.)

Once the file has completed downloading to the desktop, use the mouse to RIGHT click on the file. This will open a menu and on that menu we will click on Run as Administrator. The update will then attempt to install using the highest privileges available to a user. If no error messages appear then the update installed correctly. Restart the PC and View Update History to verify successful installation.

Sometimes we have to do it ourselves.

WINDOWS UPDATES – END OF LIFE

All good things must come to an end. Every day now I come across programs that will not install on a PC because the operating system is no longer supported. This doesn't mean the computer will stop working, it just means that new software with all its bells and whistle will not be available for use. While it may be painful and sad to know that the shiny new digital domestique we bought ten years ago has been passed by, from a support perspective we probably should know where we stand.

Regardless of the PC on the desk, use the right mouse button to click on My Computer (XP) or Computer. (Vista and Windows 7) A **context menu** will appear and at the bottom of the menu is the label Properties. Use the left mouse button to click on Properties. A new window will open. Near the top of the window it will read Windows XP Home, Vista Home, Windows 7 Home or something similar to that. If we happen to be running a business version it may have the words Professional, Ultimate or Enterprise. Just below that it may say Service Pack 1, 2 or 3 or it may not have any Service Pack listed.

Every Microsoft product has a lifecycle. The lifecycle begins when the product first goes on sale, Windows XP came to market in 2001, and ends when all support is retired for that product. Microsoft states that: "End of support refers to the date when Microsoft no longer provides automatic fixes, updates, or online technical assistance."

Over the release of different operating systems Microsoft has released what it refers to as Service Packs. These Service Packs are described by Microsoft as: "part of the process of keeping your Windows product up to date. They combine the latest updates and fixes into one package or download. A service pack can include security and performance improvements as well as support for new types of hardware." Service Packs can be downloaded manually or most folks receive them via Windows Automatic Updates.

> **Grandma and Grandpa, how come you're so smart?**
> **Context Menu:** Menus which pop up when right mouse clicking an item on a computer, offering a list of options which vary depending on the application running, and the item selected.
> All major functions plus some standard windows functions are available in a context menu.
> Context menus offer a quick mouse click to copy/paste, create shortcut and more regularly used functions.
> Wrong: The restaurant in the prison offered a context printed menu.

One advantage of making sure that our Windows OS is up to date with the latest Service Pack is that each Service Pack has its own end of support date. Example: Windows XP Service Pack 1 had its support retired October 10, 2006; Service Pack 2 ended July 13, 2010. But if we have updated our XP machine to Service Pack 3 we will continue to receive updates, patches and fixes until 2013. Vista users with Service Pack 1 will see support end this July and should upgrade to Service Pack 2 which will be supported until 2013. Windows 7 users should be at Service Pack 1 which is the current Pack.

The Service Packs are designed to address a myriad of issues that arise over time and extend the usefulness of the operating system. So what are some of the other consequences of not keeping our systems updated? One direct example is a program called Microsoft Security Essentials, a full antivirus suite provided by Microsoft for the amazing price of zero. However it will not run on any computer unless it is running at least Windows XP Service Pack 3.

The easiest way to keep our computers up to date is to turn on Automatic Updates. Windows XP users go to control panel – Automatic Updates and choose one of the options listed there. Vista and Windows 7 click on the Start button and choose Windows Updates from the list. In the dialogue box that opens click on Change Settings and from the pull down menu choose Update Automatically. To manually download and install the latest Service Packs for our machines, surf over to http://windows.microsoft.com/en-US/windows/downloads/service-packs and follow the instructions to make sure the PC has all the latest updates.

MAINTENANCE TIPS FROM MARTHA

"Court, love your columns but sometimes they are over my head, beyond my comprehension, bordering on the esoteric." Well, Martha if you think you can do better; here is the keypad and the word processing program. Go ahead and write next week's column.

Hi all, Martha here. I would feel a bit guilty if there were no column next week so I am going to take a stab at it. I have been the point of Court's scribing foil for almost three years so I should have absorbed something of value. Maybe some of the basics might fill the bill.

How about the **taskbar**? Usually it is along the bottom of the screen and contains the start button on one end and the clock and startup program icons on the other. Sometimes it has a tendency, for no apparent reason to move to one of the sides or the top of the screen. There are a few folks that prefer it at the top or side instead of the bottom. How do we move the taskbar? To move the taskbar from its default position along the bottom edge of the screen to any of the other three edges of the screen: Click a blank portion of the taskbar. Hold down the left mouse button, and then drag the mouse pointer to the place on the screen where you want the taskbar. For example, you may want the taskbar to be positioned vertically on the right side of your screen. After you move the mouse pointer to the position on your screen where you want the taskbar, release the mouse button. Remember: The taskbar can be docked on the left side, right side, top, or bottom of your screen, but you cannot move the Start button from side to side on the taskbar. If we desire the toolbar to stay where we put it, right mouse click on the taskbar and from the context menu that appears left click on Lock The Taskbar

Speaking of default. What exactly does that mean, default? Default means an option that is selected automatically unless an alternative is specified. For example: Windows puts the taskbar at the bottom of the screen (the default position) unless the user moves it specifically to another position. Another example most people have seen is when installing a program and it asks if the user wants the program installed to a default location, usually c:\program files or does the user want to specify a different location? In general, the default

> **Grandma and Grandpa, how come you're so smart?**
> **Taskbar:** Bar at the bottom of a computer screen displaying buttons showing which programs are currently running.
> We can pin icons to the taskbar to make it easy to find and launch our favorite programs.
> The taskbar also includes the START button, usually the time and date and icons for start up programs.
> Wrong: The list of jobs to do was endless and to get our assignment we walked up to the taskbar.

choice is usually satisfactory and can be safely accepted.

When starting our computer it tries to start in normal mode by default. But sometimes it is necessary to start a computer in safe mode. What is safe mode? Safe mode is primarily used to troubleshoot problems with Windows by only running the bare essentials of the Windows operating systems and device drivers. Once entering safe mode, the user can execute commands and load devices one at a time. Windows will start with a minimal configuration and generic drivers so that system errors can possibly be corrected. So how do we start our pc in safe mode? Turn on the computer. Immediately begin tapping the <F8> key. Use the arrow keys to highlight Safe Mode and press the <Enter> key. Once in safe mode we can uninstall programs, remove drivers, start system restore or even copy a file we forgot to back up if there is a chance we may lose the hard drive.

Since Court has been finding all sorts of ways to save money using the computer I thought I would pass this on as well. We know how expensive ink cartridges are and can't believe how short they seem to last. Most people use a printer to print documents, coupons, receipts, emails or other text type documents. Consider changing the default (Court, they know what that is now.) settings from normal color quality to fast draft black ink only. Normal print uses 600 x 600 dots per inch and all available colors to print. Printing a text document forces all text to print with all colors. If we change the default to fast draft black ink only, the printer uses 300 x 300 dots per inch (half as much ink) and our color cartridge can be saved for the few times we actually print a picture or some other color based print job. Every printer has this ability, just look in the printer preferences for each printer and make the appropriate setting changes.

(Court, I think I did it.)

TICK TOCK, THE IMPORTANCE OF TIME

Tick tock. Tick tock. "Time Has Come Today" sang the Chambers Brothers in 1968. Chicago harmonized with "Does Anybody Know What Time It Is?" Then followed their question with "Does Anybody Care?" Van Halen's musical entreaty was "Don't Waste My Time." In 1974 Jim Croce sang about saving Time In A Bottle. Time, is something that we either have too much of or don't have enough of. How many times have we said, "I just plain ran out of time?" Or "I didn't realize what time it was." Or my favorite, "Time just got away from me."

Tick Tock, tick tock. What is time? Time keeps everything from happening all at once. Without time we wouldn't be able to remember the past. Or for that matter, even with time, why can't we remember the future? Time also has different speeds. Time flies, or time just drags by. We even say that time stands still. Sometimes we lose time, or gain time. We give certain time specific events names such as Christmas Time or Bed Time or Lunch Time. So with all this importance placed on Time, how do we know what time it is?

Tick Tock, tick tock. Check our wristwatch. What time does it say? Now, look at the kitchen clock. Is it ahead or behind our watch? How about the clock in the dining room? Still a different time? Now look at our VCR. (there's old technology) I bet for most of us it says twelve o'clock. (Is he a mind reader Martha?) "So what," we say? Does it really matter if we are five or ten minutes late or early? Two thousand years ago, two buddies would say, meet me under the big tree at the new moon. So we would get there a few days early, camp and wait because no one could actually tell the exact moment of the new moon. Time then was plus or minus a few days. (So what are five or ten minutes?)

Do you have OnStar in your car, or GPS on your boat or on the Smartphone? Did you know that your position in the world to within a few feet is calculated by measuring the time it takes for signals to bounce from you to satellites in orbit? Stephen Dick, the United States Naval Observatory's historian, points out that each nanosecond – one billionth of a second -- of error translates into a GPS error of one foot. If the satellite time is off by the same five or ten minutes as the clocks in your house, OnStar might send your tow truck to Tampa,

> **Grandma and Grandpa, how come you're so smart?**
> **Encrypted:** To convert computer data and messages into something incomprehensible using a key, so that only a holder of the matching key can reconvert them.
> To ensure that our bank information or passwords cannot be read by outsiders it is encrypted.
> We can make a very simple substitution cipher that will encrypt our messages such as A = B and B = C.
> Wrong: All the kids in the marketplace say: walk like an Encrypted.

or Sea Tow might be looking in the Atlantic instead of Charlotte Harbor.

Even more important is the time between our computers and the computers of our banks or brokerages or any site that requires us to log on. These sites are requiring we log in because the connection between us and them is **encrypted**. Part of the encryption mechanism is time and date which can not be off more than a small amount. If it is, we can see security certificate errors or be unable to log in at all.

All right, how do I actually know what time it is? The genuine official keeper of time is the United States Naval Observatory. Here they currently have fifty-nine atomic clocks from which they calculate an average and answer Chicago's question. This is the official world time. And here is the answer to your next trivia question. Of the fifty-nine atomic clocks currently used, ten of them are hydrogen masers and forty-nine are HP-5071 cesiums. (Gesundheit!) No, I don't know what a hydrogen maser is either. But, these clocks must be accurate because it is predicted that the average of these clocks will be off by one second every six million years. So…

If you are running Windows XP, double click on the time in the lower right hand corner. A dialog box will open up and there will be a tab labeled Internet Time. Click on it and put a check in the box that is labeled automatically synchronize with an Internet Time Server. Below that you can see at least two servers listed, time.windows.com or time.nist.gov. Choose which ever you wish and let your computer set its clock with the atomic clocks and display the most accurate time currently possible. (Now go set the rest of the clocks in the house.) For those using Vista or Windows 7 click on the time in the lower right corner. A box opens displaying a calendar and a clock. At the bottom of the window is the phrase change date and time settings. Click on that link and a new dialogue box opens. There are three tabs at the top, the first tab allows us to set the time and date and the time zone we are in. The second tab is labeled additional clocks and allows us to display two clocks on the computer. For example we can set the first one to our local time and the second one to the time where are kids live, say Texas. That way when they call us at one in the morning we can look at the computer and realize it is only eleven where they live.

Until next time. And, oh by the way, don't be late.

OF MICE AND GERBILS

I know, I know, how could anything about a computer be funny? Actually there is nothing funny about a computer. However, sometimes as a computer tech, there arrives a moment with a computer user that simply screams out for something truly silly. This is my story, and I am sticking to it.

Many years ago, visiting my wife's sister and her family, they decided that since I was there, they would purchase their first computer. I went with them to a store selling computers and we picked out a very nice IBM model. This was a top of the line, 486 processor, (I always wondered 486 what?) We added a mammoth 14" monitor that took two men and a small pony to lift, and of course the flagship Microsoft Windows 95.

Once we got home, we opened the box and there it was in all its shiny glory. We carefully began to attach all the cables and surprise, surprise, didn't end up with any extra cords. Now the moment of truth. I let my sister-in-law push the power button and viola, lights came on, the monitor glowed and there in front of us was the Windows 95 desktop. (OK, there might have been a three or four minute gap from pushing the button to seeing the desktop but you get the idea.) It was a glorious moment. In one $1700 movement of cash, my sister-in-law's family had leaped into the high tech age. The world of surfing the net, email, blue screens, lockups, and an investment that in four years would be worth nothing, assuming it still worked. But then…..

My sister-in-law picked up the mouse and said, "What is this?" Now a sympathetic human would have begun the explanation of exactly how this human-machine interface device worked and why it was so important to the ease of using the computer. But a computer technician sees the world through wavy glass. "That is a gerbil," I said.

My sister-in-law was born at night but she wasn't born last night. Boring into my soul with her "You had better not be messing with me look." She proceeded to tell me that the people at her work were referring to a "**mouse**" that they used to control the computer. What to do, she obviously had some points of reference that

Grandma and Grandpa, how come you're so smart?
Mouse: Hand-operated device that controls the coordinates of a cursor on your computer screen.
A mouse will appear in the Device Manager as HID. (Human Interface Device)
A mouse can be wired or wireless, handheld or a trackball which uses less space to control the cursor.
Wrong: If the computer mouse is causing problems, it's time to get a computer cat.

had her pointed in the right direction? So, I did the only thing a good husband could do, knowing full well that anything I said would be immediately reported to my wife. (I was treading on very, very thin ice.)

I then related how, Xerox had actually developed the mouse and given it to Microsoft, (She certainly wouldn't know any better.) And that IBM used a proprietary device for moving the cursor and couldn't legally call it a mouse. Consequently, since IBM was bigger than Microsoft, (at that time it was) they called it a gerbil.

Sometimes when you tell a story like this, the person listening looks around for confirmation. My sister-in-law looked around and saw my son who also dabbled with computers at the time and she asked him if it really was a gerbil. Usually at this point life ends and you go home. But, my son simply nodded his head and said it was true. So for the rest of the weekend, I helped my sister-in-law's family learn how to use the computer, always referring to the gerbil.

Fortunately, we left that Sunday night and headed home. Monday my sister-in-law went to work and told all her coworkers about her new computer and the gerbil. Monday night our phone rang. It wasn't pretty.

Want the true skinny on the evolution of the mouse? Surf over to http://sloan.stanford.edu/MouseSite/.

There are pictures of old gerbils; I mean mice, and their predecessors.

BEEEEP, BEEEEP BACKING UP

Beeeeep…..Beeeeep…….Beeeeep. I was sitting in my bathrobe this morning, drinking a cup of coffee and reading the local rag. I mean the Charlotte Sun, when this awful noise crashed into my morning routine. Beeeeeep……Beeeeeep……Beeeeep. There it was again. I jumped up; or more accurately, got up. That early in the morning not everything wants to function quite as sprightly as it once did. I walked out the front door to see what was going on. Coming down our street in reverse was a large moving truck.

Beeeeep….Beeeeep….Beeeeep. Now I am not superstitious but this was a bit weird. Have you ever had one of those days where at the end of the day you say, "I should buy a lottery ticket?" One of those days when seemingly random events have a recurring theme embedded in them. For example: I client of mine gave me his phone number. Later that day I went to his house and his house number was the same number as the last four digits of his phone number. Then oddly enough, when setting up a broadband account, they asked him for the last four digits of his social security number and, you guessed it, it was the same number.

Beeeeeep…..Beeeeeep…….Beeeeep. So here I am standing in my driveway, listening to a truck make that terribly annoying noise and it hits me. The truck is BACKING UP. This is the second similarity in two random events. Not twelve hours prior to this, a business client of mine had called me and told me his PC had crashed during a power outage and now it would not restart. I had run over to help him but the PC was in need of a complete re-installation of the operating system. I looked up and asked for all the BACK UPS so I could rebuild the system for him. "BACK UPS, what BACK UPS?" he said. Fortunately PC CPR (that's a computer/medical term) was able to get the system **BACK UP** and limping along sufficiently to do an immediate BACK UP of all critical business information. Happy ending so far.

Beeeeeep…..Beeeeep……Beeeeeep. What was this series of events trying to tell me? As I pondered the question I turned and went BACK UP to the house. Wait a minute, is that the third event? I realized that while my PCs are all supposed to automatically BACK UP all important data, it had been awhile since I actually checked the BACK UPs myself. How do I run my BACK UPs? First, since I have more than one machine networked together, I have software on my machines that takes all the important files from one PC and copies it to the other on a regular schedule. This means that each machine on the network has a complete copy of all

> **Grandma and Grandpa, how come you're so smart?**
> **Backup:** Copying files or databases so they will be preserved in case of catastrophic failure.
> A backup means having more than one copy of critical or irreplaceable data or pictures.
> We can copy files to external hard drives, flash drives or even to online storage in the Cloud.
> Wrong: When ever I backup up there is this obnoxious beeping sound.

the important files on each machine. Lose one machine, no files are lost, and as soon as a new machine is installed, I am BACK UP and running. Second, the critical files or the ones that would be nearly impossible to recreate, are burned to CD ROM from time to time. Finally, on rare occasions I will make an image of the entire hard drive (no this does not mean I take the PC apart and take a picture of the hard drive) and store it on the network. Windows 7 now has this capability built in so third party software is no longer needed.

Now, let's BACK UP a minute. You don't have multiple PCs on a network. You don't have a CD Burner, and finally your camera doesn't take pictures of bits and bytes. When your PC crashes you want to be BACK UP right away too. What should you do? Go to http://www.skydrive.com/ and open a free Windows Live account. ("Did he say FREE, Martha?") There you can store twenty five gigs of data, (that is a lot of space) or the equivalent of about thirteen thousand copies of this book for free. Not only would your data be secured and BACKED UP, but if necessary you could access your files anywhere in the world. Other locations for free online storage are Google Docs which allows one gig for free and additional storage may be purchased and Dropbox allows two gigs for free, more at reasonable prices. Isn't the Internet wonderful?

If cloud storage isn't of interest, purchase a flash drive or external hard drive to copy files to. Remember a back up means that we have TWO copies of critical files.

Hopefully you have picked up the recurring theme embedded in the seemingly random preceding paragraphs. I have to head BACK UP to the office now, but later on, I think I will go out and buy a lottery ticket. Beeeeep......Beeeeep.......Beeeeep!

SOFTWARE AUTOMATES BACKUPS

Remember not too long ago when everyone would visit the neighbor down the street to see this new contraption called a computer? Real science fiction stuff, right from episodes of Star Trek. Here it is, only a couple decades later and many homes I visit have multiple computers. As multiple computers became common place the need to have the same file on different machines for different people to work on became a necessity. As we moved our critical information and pictures from filing cabinets and photo albums to digital format it became important to make backups of irreplaceable data by copying it to flash drives, external hard drives and other computers.

Computers in business environments often have a dedicated employee to make sure that files are backed up or synced between computers. In the home environment we often procrastinate these tasks until we lose a file or update the wrong file with information. Fortunately there is software from Microsoft that automates the task of making copies or ensuring that the same file exists on multiple computers. The two programs that can ease our tasks are Live Mesh (www.mesh.com) a Windows product and SyncToy. (www.microsoft.com/downloads and type SyncToy in the search field. SyncToy is distributed by Microsoft but is not part of Windows and therefore not supported by Microsoft Technical Support. There are multitudes of programs available that will perform the same tasks, but I like the price of these two. Zero, zip, and nada. (Martha, the price is right!)

Windows Live Mesh uses the Internet to sync files between Internet connected PCs and a Cloud based storage system called Skydrive. Mesh will automatically copy up to five **gigabytes** of data to the cloud while Skydrive itself will allow manual uploads to twenty five gigs of data. Unfortunately Mesh will not run on PCs running Windows XP. It is only available for Windows Vista, Windows 7 and Mac OS X version 10.5 or later. However Skydrive (www.skydrive.com) storage is available to almost any Internet connected PC. Setting up Live Mesh requires establishing an account and password with Microsoft to ensure security of our files and downloading a small program that runs continuously. To set up the account surf over to **www.skydrive.com**. We then instruct Mesh which folders contain files that we want to be exactly the same on all our computers and it syncs these files over the Internet. The first sync may take some time if we select folders with great numbers

---

Grandma and Grandpa, how come you're so smart?
Gigabyte: 1,000,000,000 bytes: one billion bytes.
Many people shorten gigabyte to just gig, as in my hard drive contains 500 gigs of storage space.
A DVD contains 4.2 gigs and camera memory cards can be 32 gigs or more.
Wrong: The musician looks out at the small crowd and proclaimed this gigabytes.

---

of files, but following that it will only sync files that have been added or changed which means the function takes very minimal time.

SyncToy on the other hand will run on Windows XP as well as Vista and Windows 7. It can sync files between our PC and an external drive, our PC and another PC on our home network or even sync between our PC and a flash drive. SyncToy is a very small program that installs quickly and only runs when we manually execute it or schedule it to run using the Windows Task Scheduler built into Windows. A very clear set of instructions for setting up synced folders and scheduling SyncToy to run automatically, can be found at www.howtogeek.com/howto/25046/schedule-synctoy-to-run-automatically-with-task-scheduler-in-windows-7/.

Computer, make it so.

BACKUP WITH A SYSTEM IMAGE

"What do a computer hard disk and a gerbil have in common? Their average lifespan is about 3-5 years." T.E. Ronneberg. Remember the feeling when the gerbil died? Can you imagine the sorrow when the hard disk refuses to turn and years of wedding pictures, letters to loved ones or critical emails vanish in the wink of an eye? The magic word is backup. Backup simply means that there is another copy of any items we can't afford to lose or reconstruct. Windows Vista and Windows 7 make it easier than ever to assemble that second copy.

Three types of backups should be considered. The first one takes place when we set up our shiny new calculating companion. Almost every computer comes with the ability to make recovery disks. In the dark ages, six or seven years ago, manufacturers would ship with the computer a set of disks to be used to reinstall the operating system and all the hardware drivers needed to run a specific PC. Today, to prevent the distribution of unlicensed copies of the Microsoft operating system, a mechanism is incorporated into new computers that allow owners to burn one set of recovery disks specific to that model computer. We should make these disks, usually two or three DVDs, and safely store them, hoping they will never be used.

The second type of backup relates to making copies of documents, pictures, music, e-mail, favorites and videos. Vista and Windows 7 Home Premium have built in a backup feature that can be set up to automatically store this information to an external storage drive or manually to a DVD. The Enterprise and Ultimate versions can backup to network drives as well. To access this feature, open the Control Panel and then open Backup and Restore. There is a wizard that will walk the user through setting up the backup and at the end will save the setup and start the first backup. This type of backup can be used to retrieve a file that we may have inadvertently deleted or corrupted. To restore a file go to Control Panel, Backup and Restore and click on Restore.

The third type of backup is referred to as a **System Image**. Think of a camera that takes a snapshot of the hard drive that can be projected onto either the same drive or a new. This backup is an all or nothing proposition. We cannot pull individual files such as documents or pictures from the Image. It will provide a method to restore the computer to the exact condition it was in the last time we made an Image. (our

---

Grandma and Grandpa, how come you're so smart?
System Image: A copy of the entire state of a computer system stored in non-volatile form such as a file. A system image is used to restore a computer to the exact condition it was when the image was created. When I replaced my hard drive I used an existing system image to make the new drive exactly like the old. Wrong: The spacecraft traveled past Pluto, turned and took a system image of the sun and planets.

snapshot.) If we project the Image onto our existing drive, it destroys everything on the drive and replaces it with the contents of the Image. Install a new drive, lay the Image down on the new drive and we have exactly the same computer we had before. The image is PC specific and most likely will not run on a different brand or model computer.

Vista and Windows 7 make it easy to create an image. Go to Control Panel, Backup and Restore and choose Create a System Image. We need an external drive to store the image on, any new hard drive installed must be higher capacity than the size of the image and we will need a System Repair Disk to restore the image which Windows asks if we want to make at the end of the image creation. Remember to make images regularly because they will only contain the data as of the last image made.

Have you backed up lately?

IS IT RAINING YET?

One of the most difficult things to start, besides a lawnmower, is a conversation. How many times have you been with a group of people, all standing around, looking like lost sheep and said to yourself, if only I had something to say? In the back of our mind however are the words of our mothers, "never talk about religion, politics or old courthouses." We loathe the possibility of offending someone. We need a topic that is of interest to everyone, offensive to none, and carries with it all the joys, triumphs and tragedies of the human condition.

Shakespeare said it best, "Weather, 'tis nobler in the mind to suffer the slings and arrows of outrageous fortune." (OK, maybe he used some old English spelling, but it's apparent he meant weather.) Weather is a universal theme. All are affected by it. We revel in the sunshine, lovers walk in the rain; our eyes watch the clouds moving in. All of us want to know what the weather will be tomorrow. How bad the weather is up north where the snowbirds run to escape our weather here. We love to discuss the weather that has been. I still hear people in this area using the weather of August 13th 2004 as a major topic of discussion.

Weather has a special significance to us. When we hear weather related comments like wind speed, cone of uncertainty, storm surge, longitude, latitude, forward speed, Doppler radar, etc our ears perk up. This is weather that we need to be cognizant of over the next few months. We want to hear hard figures, straight facts, no hyperbole, just numbers, raw and unadorned.

Kin Hubbard, a cartoonist, journalist and philosopher said, "Don't knock the weather; nine-tenths of the people couldn't start a conversation if it didn't change once in a while." With that in mind, I want to make sure that a pall of silence never falls over our little tropical Mayberry.

Recent headlines announced that tropical storm Arlene had reached wind speeds of forty miles an hour. Residents should be prepared for hurricane conditions. Now don't misunderstand, everyone should have his or her preparations well in hand, but come on, forty miles an hour? I have ceiling fans that generate greater wind speeds than that. Then it dawned on me that we need a source of conversation starters not tied to selling newspapers or TV slots. To that end I submit the following sites for consideration.

> **Grandma and Grandpa, how come you're so smart?**
> **Bookmark:** Link to a Web site address saved in a browser to facilitate quick access to the Web page.
> In Internet Explorer we call these links Favorites but common usage is to bookmark to our favorites.
> By organizing our bookmarks or favorites we are able to return to important web sites very quickly.
> Wrong: I placed a wet paperback on the hardwood table, when I picked it up there was a bookmark left.

Bookmark the following so they can be reached quickly and you'll never be at a loss for words at the next social gathering.

Go to http://www.ghcc.msfc.nasa.gov/. The Global Hydrology and Climate Center is a site from NASA that has weather related satellite images. They also have a project there called the Short term Prediction Research and Transition Center, SPoRT. Here we can watch storms in infrared, water vapor, and visible light images and get forty-eight hour weather prediction updates twice a day. This is an official government site.

Another site of interest is http://www.nhc.noaa.gov/. This government site issues advisories, satellite images, and the times and locations of aircraft reconnaissance flights.

Loyal column reader Charles forwarded http://flhurricane.com/ to me. This site, Central Florida Hurricane Center is a weather enthusiast maintained site. They clearly proclaim not to be an official weather site, but they have lots and lots of information, current and historical, regarding Florida weather. The site collects news stories related to current weather and provides links to many other weather related sites.

Devoted follower of Bits and Bytes, Bill sends these sites and they all have merit. Go to http://www.wunderground.com/tropical/ for lots of pictures, radar and general information. This site provides a location map showing all NEXRAD radars in the country and by clicking on a specific NEXRAD location a radar map appears displaying the current weather in that location. I clicked on the NEXRAD site in Grand Rapids and was able to maneuver the map so that it pinpointed Grand Haven, MI where my parents use to live. (I know that it is not warm and sunny there right now. That's why they needed lots of sweaters?) Another site Bill likes is http://radar.weather.gov, which has the long-range radar loop from Tampa along with many other cities around the country. It covers the entire state. Additionally, local forecasts are available by zip code. This site is also a government-operated site.

Now that we are armed with a plethora of weather information with which to add constancy and vividness to our conversation, please remember the words of Patrick Young. "The trouble with weather forecasting is that it's right too often for us to ignore it and wrong too often for us to rely on it."

On the other hand, wait five minutes and your forecast might be on the mark.

THE CAMERA NEVER LIES

A picture is worth a thousand words. There are times when words are inadequate and a picture captures everything that needs to be said. Show a picture at a family gathering of Aunt Martha with a lampshade on her head, and everyone understands what you are trying to say.

The camera never lies. A camera captures only what it is pointed at. It asks for no direction, nor conditions, nor implications, it simply records reality. It doesn't enlighten the viewer as to the interpretation of the image, leaving each of us to fabricate our own elucidation. "You can't fool the lens," is another axiom that emphasizes the infallibility of the camera to record reality.

The camera never lies. Or does it? How many times have you heard "the camera adds ten pounds," or "he doesn't photograph well?" Perhaps Ansell Adams, a famous photographer, said it best. "You don't take a photograph, you make it." Did he have a premonition of the future mixture of photography and computers? In the movie "Forrest Gump" there is a picture of Forrest (played by Tom Hanks) shaking hands with President John F. Kennedy. That is the message of the picture. But keep in mind that Forrest Gump is an imaginary figure and Tom Hanks was only nine years old when Kennedy was President.

The camera never lies. Truly it doesn't. However a computer doesn't see through a lens. What the computer sees in a photograph is a very small dot of color called a **pixel**. Depending on the resolution of the photo, the number of pixels can range as high as several million dots. A computer has the ability to manipulate each and every one of these dots. Take some out, move some around, add some from another picture and reality becomes whatever we wish it to be.

Let's use an old photo of our great grandparents. The photo is faded, cracked and missing a torn corner. First we use a digital scanner to convert the picture from paper and ink to a digital format. This is what allows us to see the individual pixels in the photograph. Since the photo is black and white, we will choose the GIF format. GIF is the acronym for Graphics Interchange Format. There are other formats, such as JPEG, BMP,

Grandma and Grandpa, how come you're so smart?
Pixel: Dot of light that is the basic unit from which images on computer or television screens are made.
The pixels that make up a computer screen are either, red, blue or green.
The small size of pixels makes them almost invisible to the naked eye.
Wrong: Tinkerbelle was a pixel that never left Peter Pan's side.

EPS, TIFF and many more. Each has a strength that allows for better control of some condition of the picture such as color or depth but for this example a GIF will do what we wish. We send the scanned photo to any one of a number of programs that specialize in pixel manipulation. Programs such as HP Photo Creations, (FREE) http://www.hp.com/global/us/en/consumer/digital_photography/free/software/photo-creations.html, or ACDsee 14, www.acdsystems.com, ($80) or the 800 pound gorilla, Adobe Photoshop CS5, www.adobe.com. ($700) There are many others but for the most part they work much like a word processing program from the standpoint that pixels can be copied, pasted, deleted, added, colored, moved or many other functions.

Back to our photo. We can choose to increase contrast, which reduces the fading effect. We then can recolor the photo with different tones of black and white nearly eliminating the fading. Next we zero in on the crack and use a blending effect to bring the pixels on either side of the crack into the area defined by the crack. This changes the crack pixels from white to that of the pixels on either side of it making the crack disappear. Finally, we find an area of the photo that is similar to what the torn away area would have been. We tell the program to copy an area big enough to replace the missing part and paste it into that missing area. For fun we tell the program to add a sepia tone effect to the whole picture and then send it to the printer where we have some high quality photo paper waiting. There before our eyes, is a photograph that rivals the original of ninety years ago.

The camera never lies. The techniques used to repair a photo can be used to modify or even create a picture. The same holds true for video. For example, my parents took hours and hours of eight-millimeter movies back in the late fifties and sixties. Later, Dad had it put on VHS. Hours and hours of it. Some of it is quite interesting and poignant. Some however, like when they stuck the camera out a car window and filmed miles of fields, that no one remembers why or where it was, makes for very boring viewing. However, as I digitize the film by output cables from the VCR to my computer, I can easily remove any segments that are extraneous, put in voiceovers, change sequence, use fade outs and fade-ins, add cartoon balloon comments and end up with some very interesting video. This video can then be burned to a DVD and played on the TV. I used a program called Dazzle DVD Recorder HD, http://www.pinnaclesys.com, ($50) to do this and again it is nothing more than electronic cut and paste.

So dig out those old photos, open that box of VHS tape, and go to the attic and get the cans of eight-millimeter film and make the past what you remember it to be.

Remember, the camera never lies, at least when we control the final product.

PLAY THAT FUNKY MUSIC

A social night out breaks our daily monotony every once in awhile. It may be for dinner, a few drinks, to socialize with our friends or some private event we have been invited to. Most of the time entertainment is involved in some way or another. In Charlotte County we have a plethora of venues to pick from. There are the local neighborhood bars, such as The Celtic Ray, Beef O'Brady's or the pizza place down the street. For lodge members there are The American Legion, The VFW Post, The Elks Club, The Moose Club, The Eagles and The Knights of Columbus. On any given night there are a multitude of private parties for weddings, graduations, birthdays, anniversary's or the second Tuesday of the month. (OK, I made that one up)

By now you may be asking what all these events have in common and what are they doing in a computer column. Each of these venues usually offers some form of musical entertainment on any given day of the week. Today, most musicians use a computer for more than making a list of their songs or drawing up contracts. Most of the time there will be a small ensemble (usually one or two musicians) that sounds like a small jazz band, a rock and roll band or a full orchestra. (How can that be Martha?)

They achieve that full band sound by utilizing a computer, available composing software and then emulate the missing instruments. Musicians may add Drums, Bass, Guitar, Piano, Strings, Horn Sections, or any other instrument needed to fill out a song including sound effects. Single performers may use a computer to enhance a performance while playing a lead line on a harmonica or other instrument. Musicians may pre-record a verse or the chorus of a song in a computer to provide background harmonies for the melodies they want to sing. Then the pre-recorded music is enhanced in the computer using fairly inexpensive software, converted to a format such as **MIDI** (Musical Instrument Digital Interface) and played back at the appropriate time in the song. Software can be used to raise the pitch of a voice if the notes are falling a bit flat. It can be used to clean up part of a song where two or more instruments may be conflicting or muddying up the sound. The musician can tweak the various sounds and tracks until the desired effect is achieved.

Grandma and Grandpa, how come you're so smart?
MIDI: Musical instrument digital interface, a standard adopted by the electronic music industry for controlling devices, such as synthesizers and sound cards that emit music.
Many musicians use MIDI connections with instruments to provide their own backgrounds to their songs. Using MIDI, an artist can digitize music and then manipulate it as to pitch, speed, tone and other qualities. Wrong: The style for ladies in the 1970s was to be seen wearing MIDI dresses.

One software package actually uses real recordings of top studio Jazz/Rock/Country drummers. These are not samples tracks, but are full recordings, lasting from 1 to 8 bars, playing along in perfect sync with other tracks. For example, choose a brushes style drum sound, and you will now hear lush Jazz brushes. The results are dramatically better than previous artificial drum tracks. They sound like a real drummer, because they are recordings of a real drummer.

Only a short time ago, this level of sophistication was offered to musicians recording in multi million dollar studios. Now it is available to the local musician at a reasonable cost. For a look at some software that can make this magic happen, surf over to http://www.pgmusic.com/bandbox.htm for a program called Band in a Box ($129 for the starter version) or continue on to http://www.cakewalk.com/sonar and look at SONAR X1 Studio. ($149 for the English version) I had the opportunity to watch a local musician (Just For Fun, www.justforfunband.com) record and create sixteen tracks for a song they were going to perform using Sonar. It was amazing to hear the results.

Today it is possible to record the next big hit song on a home computer and create graphics for a CD and jewel case. Burn either a master CD to send to a replication house for copies to be made or make the copies at home on a low cost DVD Duplicator. Use a home computer to connect to the Internet and create a web page that includes original music. A web site can reach many more people than a local music gig could hope to achieve. Innovative music can also be placed on various web sites that promote Indie (independent) music. It is not beyond the realm of possibilities for a producer to visit your web site, hear your music and transform you into the next American Idol. So, lay down the boogie and play that funky music till you die.

Let me know where you're playing and don't forget the tip jar.

THE COMPUTER CAN MAKE YOU A STAR

In the beginning music was made from an old log covered in animal hide for a drum beat and a piece of cat gut stretched between the ends of a bowed tree branch and plucked for a melodic instrument. This was great for appeasing the Gods around a fire after a good meal of Tyrannosaurus Rex but it just doesn't cut it in today's world.

Today, utilizing our computer we can sound like a full orchestra, a jazz combo, a rock group or any other musical combination we choose. Gone are the days of 2-inch tape and a million dollar recording studio to record the next great classic. Today we can use our computer and produce the music in our bedroom or garage.

Remember that great old song Ghost Riders In The Sky? Many artists recorded that song written by Stan Jones over the years. Some of them were Eddy Arnold, Gene Autry, Johnny Cash, Bing Crosby, Duane Eddy, Lorne Greene, Tom Jones, Frankie Laine, Dean Martin, The Outlaws, The Ventures and I think the Blues Brothers should have used this song in their movie "The Blues Brothers", instead of Rawhide.

So what does that have to do with computers and music? Go to www.musicrobot.com and search for Ghost Riders In The Sky. There you will find over 100 sites that offer that song for download, some good, some not so good. They will all be in MIDI file format. For folks nascent to music and computers, MIDI is the way computers talk to instruments and is the acronym for Musical Instrument Digital Interface. This format also allows a computer to talk to its internal sound card to produce musical sounds. Programs like Band In A Box by PG Music www.pgmusic.com allow you to type in a chord progression (either self created or from a music book) choose a style you want that song to play in and voila, you have music you can sing to or play along with.

If you play an instrument you can mute that particular instrument and "Play with the Band". More sophisticated **programs** allow you to record multiple instruments and vocals to your hard drive and burn the finished product to a CD. Bands made up of only two people can sound like an orchestra by playing along with

Grandma and Grandpa, how come you're so smart?
Programs: A sequence of instructions written to perform a specified task with a computer.
A word processing program is designed to facilitate the writing of letters, flyers, signs etc.
To use a program on a computer, the program must be installed on the computer.
Wrong: When my mother's mother joined the NFL she became a ProGram.

their computer. One such local band is called Just For Fun. Go to their web page, www.justforfunband.com, and click on the Sample Tunes button to hear an example of that technique.

Would you like to restore those old LP records or tapes in the attic? Programs are available to do just that. With the correct equipment it is possible to take an old record or tape, be it cassette, reel to reel, 8 track or ADAT and turn it into a CD. The production quality will be directly proportional to the quality of the original. There are numerous tricks that can be played (no pun intended) on the original to enhance the sound quality and usually the annoying background noise, pops, clicks and tape hiss can be removed.

Scan some old pictures of your band from long ago and make a CD label and Jewel case insert to convince people you were once a star. Take an old live recording with some crowd noise and add applause, edit out the time between songs and completely remove the songs that don't sound as good as you remember. Those were usually the ones at the end of the night when everyone (including the band) had a few rum & cola's in them.

So dust off that organ that's been sitting in the den, pull out that guitar or banjo in the closet, get that violin out of the case, limber up your fingers on that accordion, hammer the strings on that dulcimer and play along with Ghost Writers In The Sky. (What did he say Martha? Oh just ignore him, I think he has had one too many rum & cola's in him)

GUY THINGS

Guy things. Everybody knows there are certain things that despite equal rights and political correctness are still associated with guys. These things may vary from place to place but they are recognizable to anyone that happens to take notice. For example, the garage is generally considered a guy's place. The floor jack is a guy thing. Some would argue that the TV remote is a guy thing. Usually the lawnmower is a guy thing.

There are also things considered to be girl things. These things too may vary from place to place but as with guy things they are recognizable as girl things when observed. Examples are a closet full of shoes, or frilly doilies on the furniture. Even the furniture is generally considered the realm of the woman in the home. Yes, I stipulate that there are exceptions to every example given, but looking at it from a distance we know it to be true.

In my office there is a **network** of computers, all working hard to help me do what I do. They are connected to the internet, each one has specific functions, perform scheduled tasks and when asked, even entertain, educate, or clarify what ever I am working on at the time. My office is without question a guy room.

At the other end of our home is a room that used to be a bedroom. It was conscripted a few years back as a sewing room. Or perhaps (cue the scary music) more accurately a quilting room. There are sewing machines, cutting tables, plastic bins of material, tools and weapons I can't even describe but according to my wife, no quilter would be caught dead without them. And by the way, I stand corrected, it is Quilter, capital Q not quilter. This is undeniably a girl room and one that I refuse to enter except in the event of an emergency.

For several years now these two rooms have been like separate countries. The borders inviolate. Entry to either was by invitation only. But now comes the nineth biennial Disconnected Piecers Quilt Guild quilt show at the Charlotte Harbor Event Center of which my wife is one of the organizers. This means she is tasked with not only preparing some of her quilts for display, but contacting vendors, registering participants, logging in

> **Grandma and Grandpa, how come you're so smart?**
> **Network:** A collection of hardware components and computers interconnected by communication channels that allow sharing of resources and information.
> Setting up a home network allows multiple computers to share the Internet connection and printers.
> The Internet is a giant network linking any Internet capable device, computers, phones, printers and TV's.
> Wrong: To catch bait fish requires the fisherman to perform a lot of network.

entries and arranging for supplies. How can she do all this and get it ready by the show date of February 24th? You guessed it. Like an invading horde she moves into my office and fires up one of the computers that now becomes quilt central control.

She fires up MS Access and prepares databases of entries and registrants. Excel spread sheets fly from the printer with vendor positions and products. MS Word is sucking ink from the printer with the number of confirmation letters being sent out. MS Publisher is creating show fliers, brochures and press releases. Emails fly through cyberspace at lightning speed.

My computers miss me. I briefly consider a counter attack that would invade her quilting room, but a glance through the door at the tons of material, binding, fat quarters (Martha, is that like thirty cents?) quilt hangers, pillow cases, and other unknown items and I am afraid.

Now an even more horrifying event takes place in my guy room. She begins to create labels and prints them off so she can sew them into the quilts she is working on. Can you believe my computers, my links with the world, my contacts with other computer techs have been reduced to preparing pieces of a quilt? It doesn't stop there. Now she is printing off designs she has created on MY computers onto fabric and making them part of her quilts. Does that mean MY computers have become quilters? Say it isn't so.

But the worst is yet to come. I come home one evening and find my wife in the office, peering intently at a monitor, and I ask what is so fascinating. She excitedly tells me that she just used MY computer to purchase over the internet something called the Ultimate Box. First I thought she had bought herself a computer to use in HER room. Imagine my angst when she explained that the Ultimate Box was a device to be hooked up to MY computers that would allow her to take quilt designs from around the world, download them from the internet to MY computer and then into the Ultimate Box which would convert them to a format that could be read by HER SEWING MACHINE so she could sew even more elaborate quilts and win even more ribbons and awards. There will be my office network, several PC's and a sewing machine, all talking happily to each other.

Guy things, if only they truly were.

HOW MANY CAN YOU MAKE?

For just a moment, close your eyes and try to remember everything in the house that you think is there. Go room by room and try to conjure up in your mind exactly what is there. (Yes, I know it is hard to read the column with your eyes closed.) Now, open your eyes and look around. Were you as amazed as I was at all the things about that you could not think of? I noticed that junk, pictures, knick-knacks, and stuff just seem to appear. Where last week there was an empty corner, now there are two flea market metal sculptures. (I use the term sculptures, because that term is acceptable by this newspaper and the term that really describes them is not.) Where does it all come from? Or better yet, what to do with it?

This quandary raised its head the other day when for one reason or other I opened my liquor cabinet. Now before all the prohibitionists out there start their lectures, please realize that I use the contents of the liquor cabinet for medicinal purposes only. But what was surprising was that for the first time in a long time, I actually looked in the medicine, sorry, liquor cabinet. Based on the health of the folks in my home, I anticipated that there would be only two bottles in the cabinet. Specifics of the contents shall remain a secret. Imagine my surprise when I counted forty-four bottles in the cabinet. (Did he say party, Martha?) Most of them were unopened, and the ones that were opened still had most of their contents behind the cap. As I perused through the bottles, I realized that I would never drink the vast majority of these substances.

Where did all this stuff come from? Much of it is from guests that brought a bottle of their favorite poison as a house gift. Others were bottles I bought because of the proclivities of specific guests I had invited to visit my home. So there they sit. Do I throw them out? Give them away? Hire a bartender? I don't even know what most of it is used in or with. So there in lies the dilemma.

Bartenders have always fascinated me. How anyone could remember all the recipes for every drink ever thought of is a feat of mental gymnastics that is truly a gift. Sometimes, listening to some of the drinks ordered by folks at a bar, I wonder if the bartender simply makes them up as he goes. I certainly don't know the difference and I doubt the customer does either. Names such as Blue Shark, Egghead, (Maybe that one is for **computer geeks**?) Gentle Ben, (Why would a drink be named after a TV character?) and even Zoot. (Don't

---

Grandma and Grandpa, how come you're so smart?
Computer geeks: A computer expert or enthusiast.
When our computers go on the blink we call a computer geek to fix it.
Several levels of computer geeks exist such as our grandchildren, next door neighbor or a professional.
Wrong: The computer geek was the star attraction at the circus.

have a clue.)

As I visit with folks, one thing I hear over and over is, "My (son, nephew, grandchild, next door neighbor etc) is a computer whiz." It dawns on me that there is a huge market of computer geeks that would be open to job related consumable liquids. I would therefore like to offer some aspiring bartender these names for drinks yet to be created. Surely some delicious beverages could be marketed under monikers like, Megabyte, or Defrag, System Crash, or a sure seller, Memory Dump. And for the folks that only imbibe for medicinal purposes such as myself, think of the sales potential for a drink called Antivirus.

But all this doesn't solve the problem of forty-four bottles in my cabinet. Thankfully the Internet offers us a unique method to address this problem. (No you cannot sell liquor on EBay.) Go to http://www.barbug.com/barbug/bbOnhand.asp. At this site there is a list of all the most common things found in a liquor cabinet. In addition there is a list of items that may be found in other cabinets and your refrigerator. After checking off all the items that you have in the house, there is a great big button that says How Many Drinks Can I Make Right Now, click it and the site generates a list of the drinks that can be made from the ingredients on hand. It also gives you the recipe for each and everyone. In my case I have 173 different drinks to make and taste.

Cheers!

TRY SPYBOT - AND CALL ME IN THE MORNING

I have a friend of mine that many, many years ago, operated a bicycle store in a small town in the Midwest. One evening as we were discussing the previous ventures we had tried, he proceeded to tell me that one of the reasons he was successful in the bicycle business was that he gave away a spoke wrench with every bicycle purchased. This spoke wrench cost him about a dollar fifty. Which, considering the time that has passed since then, was a pretty good premium. So I asked him, what was it about the free spoke wrench that made him successful?

"People cannot resist trying to use the spoke wrench," he said. People just don't know what they are doing, but that doesn't stop them from trying. They would inevitably break a spoke or get the wheel out of round and amazingly show up back at the bicycle shop and need their wheel straightened. This provided a steady stream of repair jobs for the slow times.

How many times have you decided that you can fix something yourself, and that the so-called trained professional simply paid his tuition and gathered his experience for nothing?

So, since I have a few spare appointments open for the next week or two, I am going to give you a free spoke wrench. (Figuratively speaking.)

The most intense battle going on in the computer world right now is how to direct you to the places on the web that others want you to see. You have heard the terms, spyware, **malware** and many others. Without going into a deep explanation of what they are, suffice it to say that these entities send you pop ups, pop unders, spam and in severe cases actually hijack your PC forcing you to go to sites that you would never (well most of you would never) voluntarily go. In addition, if you have enough of these entities on your machine, it will actually slow down and even freeze up. Now, here is your free spoke wrench.

> **Grandma and Grandpa, how come you're so smart?**
> **Malware:** Short for malicious software; consists of programming designed to disrupt or deny operation, gather information that leads to loss of privacy or exploitation.
> Malware such as fake anti virus programs try to trick us into giving them our credit card numbers.
> An antivirus program, strong passwords and personal vigilance will prevent malware from infecting a PC.
> Wrong: The men's store downtown carries a fine selection of malware.

Go to http://www.safer-networking.org/en/index.html and download Spybot Search and Destroy. This program will search your entire computer for the little buggers I previously mentioned and remove them from your machine. This program is Freeware. This means that you don't HAVE to pay for it. However, if you want the gentleman who has made it his life mission to wipe out spyware to continue, then please send him a donation. Some of you will carefully read all the details on how the program works, what to do with it, and the potential problems that may or could be caused by not following the directions. To you, I salute and good hunting. Your computer will now be inhabited by fewer of the little nasties. Those who don't read the details, a computer tech can fix what you break.

Why do people create these insidious, perverse adware, spyware and malware programs? Pure and simple, MONEY. These things are actually little programs that are placed on your PC, often without your knowledge but more often with your uninformed knowledge. They are designed to put something in front of your eyes, an ad, or a chance to win something, or even sometimes to scare you into buying something. One of the most effective ones out there gives you a pop up window that looks very important and states that your computer may contain spyware. If your CD Rom drawer opens, then you are infected and please press the Buy Now button for some super duper monster spyware killer. The CD Rom drawer opens just as predicted and you click on the button. Please give your credit card number to them and you will be charged only $79.95 for this wonderful program. The fact of the matter is, they now have your credit card number and you just downloaded a program that will insure that you have a never ending supply of pop ups and spam. They infest a couple of hundred million PC's with this little scam and maybe only one percent respond, and they just retired to Tahiti.

What are the symptoms of an infested PC? First, it will seem to take longer and longer to start up. Second, the pc will seem to run slower and slower. And finally, the PC will freeze up and be non responsive.

Interestingly, I exhibit a lot of these symptoms myself, as I get older. I wonder if they sell a human version of Spybot at the drugstore?

PROGRAMS UP TO DATE? PSI LETS US KNOW

Do we know how many programs are on our PC? Two? Ten? Thirty? Do we even need to be aware of how many programs are loaded on the computer? Yes, we should be aware. We should be aware simply because, unless we have purchased a computer and never hooked it to the Internet, or loaded any additional software, our calculating companion is in a state of constant change. Some examples folks are familiar with are the seemingly constant updates by our anti virus program and regular updates for Windows. They represent only the tip of the iceberg. Java, Adobe, Skype, Flash are just a few of the myriad of programs that most of us have loaded on our digital devices. A recent survey of my own electronic savant revealed ninety-five programs that were loaded, not necessarily running, but available for use should they be needed.

Companies that write software for computer users know that changes on our computers can cause their software to operate outside normal parameters. Consequently, reputable companies will make updates and/or **patches** available to keep their software up to date and functional. There may also be software that has reached end of life. This is software that is simply so old that there is no longer any support by the manufacturer and as time goes by the odds increase that the software may stop working. There are also nefarious characters roaming the net, just looking and probing for weaknesses in software that will allow them to exploit our PC for their gain and our loss. Certainly the Windows OS is a favorite target but many of the second tier software programs can offer an easy access point. Because of software environment changes, end of life and malware attacks, it is important to keep programs resident on our logical workstation updated.

While surveying and inventorying all the software and it's current state on a PC may seem a daunting task, there is another piece of software available that will do just that for us, give a detailed report of the software on our computer and it's current state in terms of end of life or available updates. The program is Secunia Personal Software Inspector. (PSI) Best of all, it is FREE. (Martha, my favorite word.)

How does it work? According to Secunia, "The Secunia PSI works by examining files on your computer (primarily .exe, .dll, and .ocx files). These files contain non-specific meta information provided by the software vendor only. This data is the same for all users, and originates from the installed programs on your computer -

> **Grandma and Grandpa, how come you're so smart?**
> **Patch:** Software designed to fix problems with, or update a computer program or its supporting data. When a security vulnerability or operational problem is found in software, a patch may be issued to fix it. Many times a patch provides a temporary fix until a more encompassing update or service pack is issued. Wrong: When my pant leg caught the edge of the computer and tore, I immediately sewed a patch on it.

never from their configuration. Please read the privacy statement available at the bottom of this page and through the Secunia PSI application for more details about how information from your computer is used by Secunia. After examining all the files on your local hard drive(s), the collected data is sent to Secunia's servers, which match the data against the Secunia File Signatures engine (https://psi.secunia.com/) to determine the exact applications installed on your system. This information can then be used to provide you with a detailed report of the missing security related updates for your system."

Fire up the computer and surf over to secunia.com/PSISetup.exe. The current version is Version 2.0. Click on the Run button when asked to start the install. This will start the PSI Setup wizard that will walk us through the installation. Accept the license agreement, click next. Decide if PSI should auto update itself or if we will run the update occasionally, then click next. Next choose whether we want a tray icon for PSI or not, click next, read the READ ME text, click next and then click Install. When the install is done, click finish. PSI will then ask if it should launch PSI now. No time like the present. PSI now runs a scan and when finished on Scan Results. PSI now displays end of life programs, programs missing updates and a list of all the programs on our computer. Any programs with missing updates can be updated right from the list.

Just another gizmo for the digital toolbox.

WHAT'S ON THE PC? BELARC KNOWS

Let us discuss nightmares. I am not talking about the kind of nightmare that occurs in your sleep. I am talking about the kind, which after it occurs the thought runs through your head, I should have (fill in the blank). For example, several years ago I had a flat tire. I knew the tire was worn, and I knew it should be replaced, and even better, I had actually started pricing tires. I just hadn't replaced it yet. So there I was, forced to buy a tire immediately, a tow charge and great inconvenience. I should have ...

But I realize that all of you are well prepared for any catastrophe. You went out and bought extra flashlights and batteries, a couple of gallons of bottled water, some candles, blankets, a battery powered radio and even a generator. Stocked the pantry with a few weeks worth of non-perishable food and prepared a plan to evacuate if necessary. Of course, I did all this AFTER the hurricane. I should have ...

With all this planning, let me ask you a question. What would happen if your computer, or a program on it quit? What would you do? Call your eight-year-old child? Ask your neighbor for help? Do you know all your passwords? Do you know where all the disks are that came with the programs? Better yet, where are the **product keys** for all the software? (the little orange tags with numbers that fell off the plastic CD ROM jewel case) Are your files backed up? Do you have the number of a good computer tech?.

In addition to the programs on the computer, there are also specific drivers (little programs that instruct a device how to react to commands) for the video, audio, printers, keyboard, network card, modem etc. Do you know which drivers will work with your computer? Sure, you can download new drivers from the Internet, but not if you don't know which one is needed. How about the motherboard? Who manufactured it and which model. Do you know which version of the BIOS (Basic Input Output System) is required for that motherboard?

Bad things do happen to good computers. Rest assured though, that they will only happen at the most inopportune time. When a bad thing does happen, do you really want to say, "I should have...? A little bit of

> **Grandma and Grandpa, how come you're so smart?**
> **Product Key:** A usually unique, alphanumeric code required by software programs during installation to ensure that each copy of their software was legally purchased.
> Many software manufactures place a tag on the CD case containing the product key for that software.
> If I lose the product key I will not be able to reinstall that software without buying another copy.
> Wrong: I love to spend a weekend in Product Key, Florida.

planning can save the day.

Passwords should be written down and stored in a safe place. Sure, you told Windows to remember all the passwords and it does a great job of it, until Windows isn't working anymore. Additionally, in Windows XP, Vista and Windows 7 consider password protecting you primary account and activating the Guest account. That way when your grandchild visits let them use the Guest account. When they change the password to the Guest account without telling anyone what it is, you can use the Primary account to get in and reset the Guest account password. I have one client that calls me every year after the grandchild leaves because they cannot logon to the computer. (Love those grandkids)

Program disks should be stored in the cases or wrappers. Do not use them as coasters or Frisbees. Make sure that the little stickers with the product keys are with them. Consider using a Sharpie marker to print the key on the disk itself. I am convinced that the software makers have a secret glue formula for those stickers so that they fall off after a certain period of time. Without the product key, the software cannot be reinstalled and you need to buy a new copy of it.

Now go to http://www.belarc.com and download Belarc Advisor. This is a free program that runs a complete inventory list of the entire computer's hardware, along with the manufactures name and model number. This is important when it comes to loading the correct drivers for each item. Belarc also displays the make and model of the computer along with the motherboard and the version of the BIOS. As they say on TV, and that's not all! Belarc will list all the programs on your computer, where they are installed and the license and product keys. As a bonus, it will show not only the operating system and service pack level, but also all the Windows Hotfixes and whether or not they need to be reinstalled.

Print out this information and put it in a safe place along with the program and computer installation disks. Do it now, while the computer is working well. Never utter the words, I should have ….

HANDY TOOLS AT OUR FINGERTIPS

We often hear the myth that people only use ten percent of their brains. The supposition is that if we used the other ninety percent we could do amazing things, maybe even utilize psychic powers. When it comes to our calculating companions I wonder if many of us use even ten percent of its potential. Here are some capabilities available right beneath our fingertips.

Windows 7 is loaded with features for assisting the user with day to day tasks. Take a look at the calculator. It can be found by clicking the Start button and typing Calc or Start - Accessories – Calculator. The calculator built into Windows 7 looks just like the calculator in Vista until we explore the View menu at the top of the calculator. For the brainiacs there are Scientific and Programmer modes that display information such as sin, cos, hex and Qword. For less esoteric needs we can find Unit Conversion on the menu. Can't remember how many pints in a gallon? Plug in the number of gallons and ask for pints. The answer appears. Temperature conversions, energy, area, time and more are all available. Under the View menu there is a Date calculation which computes the number of days or weeks between two dates, a very useful tool for clubs and groups providing members with a countdown to upcoming events. And the last item on the View menu is called Worksheets and consists of tools to quickly calculate mortgage payments, lease payments and fuel economy.

A tool that seems particularly useful for saving a little time is found just above the Start button when we click on it. There is a field called the **Start Menu Search Box** that we can type in. Start to type the name of a program or document, that program or document appears in the list above and we can click on it if there are more than one or if only one item appears in the list, hit the enter key and that item opens. Beats clicking on the Start button – All Programs – program folder if we can find it and then the program itself. When typing in the box consider that less is more. Calc will bring the calculator up just as would typing the entire word.

Our digital domestique also recognizes that we humans suffer from serious memory loss. To help us remember our assigned upcoming tasks, Windows 7 provides a cute program called Sticky Notes. Click on Start and type Sticky in the search field. A notepad appears that looks just like the sticky notes we have plastered all over our desks and refrigerators. These notes appear on our screen and we can type important reminders in

Grandma and Grandpa, how come you're so smart?
Start Menu Search Box: Allows finding programs and files on the computer by typing in search terms. Click Start and type all or part of the name of a program or file to have Windows take you right to it. The Start Menu Search Box will also search on the Internet if we need it to in order to find information. Wrong: At a restaurant I often start with the menu and search for a box lunch.

them. If we right mouse click on them we can even color code them for any purpose. Click on the + button in the title bar of a Sticky Note and a new note appears for that next required task. (Martha, the entire screen is covered with Sticky Notes.)

If any program begins misbehaving under Windows click Start, type PSR and press Enter. The Problem Step Recorder (PSR) will open a control module on the Desktop. Click Start Record. Now repeat the steps leading up to the problem and the Problem Steps Recorder will record every click and key stroke. It will take screen grabs (pictures of what is on the screen), and when we finally click on End Recording, package everything up into a zipped (compressed) MHTML file. The control module then opens a dialog box that allows us to give the file a name and save it where we can locate it later. We can send an e-mail to our favorite tech, attach the PSR file, then the tech can actually see what led up to the problem and any error messages that appeared. PSR will save hours of troubleshooting time.

Windows 7 also offers one other tool for less severe problems. Click on the Start button, then Control Panel and click on Troubleshooting. Microsoft includes a suite of Troubleshooters that can automatically try to resolve certain types of problems. Troubleshooters are available to fix program compatibility issues, hardware problems, resolve Internet connection tribulations and perform maintenance and performance tasks.

There are many useful tools built into Windows 7 that can serve our needs. Explore!

COMMAND PROMPT: GET TO THE HEART OF THE PROBLEM

Computers have come to be a mainstay of our lives because they are easy to use. The secret to ease of use is referred to as **GUI**. (Graphical User Interface) Computers today operate by finding a picture that corresponds to something we want to do, we click on it and our wishes are fulfilled. A few years ago, a user would type lines of commands into the computer to get desired results. Some folks remember this as the DOS days. (Disk Operating System) There were quite a few different flavors of DOS with MS-DOS used in Windows 95, 98 and Millennium.

Windows XP, Vista and Windows 7 have a slightly different form of DOS that can be called up via the CMD.exe program. It looks like DOS and functions by typing in commands that perform certain tasks. Some of the commands can have profound or damaging results if a user is unfamiliar with these actions. However there are very useful commands that can help diagnose problems, perhaps fix problems, or provide useful information.

To open the CMD dialogue box, (Windows XP) click on the START button – Run and type cmd in the search box and click OK. Vista and Windows 7 users click on the Start button and in the search box directly above the button type cmd and hit Enter on the keyboard. A black box will open and it will have some lines of text that look something like c:\users\username> with a cursor flashing behind it.

Let's try some useful commands. Sometimes we open our Internet browser and get the infamous Page cannot be displayed. Use CMD to narrow down the problem. Open the CMD window and type in, (ping www.google.com). If we are not connected to the Internet this command will return several lines of text stating that the destination host is unreachable. This would indicate that the problem is with the router, modem or our Internet provider. But if the return is something like Reply from and a series of numbers then we are connected to the Internet and the problem resides with the browser.

> **Grandma and Grandpa, how come you're so smart?**
> **GUI (Graphical User Interface):** Allows users to interact with electronic devices with images rather than text commands.
> A graphical user interface (GUI) commonly pronounced gooey, made the computer usable for the masses. The computer desktop is one example of a graphical user interface.
> Wrong: When baking a wet bottom shoe fly pie the molasses filling is particularly GUI.

Type in ipconfig and a window full of data will be returned. Look for the line that reads IPv4 and a series of numbers similar to 192.168.1.100. This represents the address of our digital domestique on the Internet. However if the first three numbers are 169 then we are looking at the IP number of the PC's network adaptor indicating some type of hardware or driver problem.

Another interesting command is TREE. This command will list all the files and folders on the drive. It will be a very long list but we can scroll up or down is we are looking for something in particular.

If the operating system itself is crashing or not operating as we think it should, another command from the CMD window that can be useful is sfc /scannow. (System File Checker) The System File Checker tool (SFC.exe) scans for missing or corrupted system files and repairs them. However to run this command in Vista/Windows 7 click the start button, type CMD in the search box. When CMD is listed in the start menu, right mouse click on it and from the context menu click on Run as Administrator. This opens CMD with elevated rights. Type at the prompt: sfc /scannow.

We are on a roll now. Open a CMD window with elevated rights (Run as Administrator) and type chkdsk /f. The chkdsk command, often referred to as check disk, is used to identify and correct certain hard drive errors. Chkdsk cannot run on a system that is in use so a message will appear asking if we want to schedule chkdsk to run after the next restart. Type yes and close the window. The next time we restart the computer Chkdsk will run first then start Windows.

A picture isn't always worth a thousand words.

127.0.0.1 NO PLACE LIKE HOME

When I was fourteen or fifteen, a friend of mine and I decided to hike the Horseshoe Trail. We got turned around and found ourselves lost. We stopped at an Amish farmhouse for directions to Zinn's Diner which was just down the road from where we were camping. We didn't know the address of the campground or the diner but figured everyone knew where we wanted to go. The farm owner, dressed in black trousers, grey shirt, black vest and a straw hat, stood for a moment pulling on his beard and then began to tell us how to get to Zinn's diner.

"Go down to the big oak tree on Amos's drive, turn right …..no, no." He ponders a moment more and says, "Cut across Braeder's field here until you get to the big cement road and then….. no, no." Again he thinks for a moment and says, "Go down to Jake's Suzie's Mary's white house and turn left ….no, no." Finally, he looks up at us and says, "You can't get there from here."

How important is an address? Every single place has an address. The Internet acts the same way. Every computer or device connected to the Internet has a unique address. In computereze this address is referred to as a device's **IP address**. (Internet Protocol) For example, right now my address is 68.56.202.94 on the Internet. If we dial in or connect via a broadband connection, we are assigned an IP address. This address is our place in the World Wide Web.

But wait a minute. You've never been to a place on the Internet called 65.56.202.94. Because it is difficult to remember numbers, we assign names to sites on the Internet. For example, my website is www.bitsandbytesonline.com. To make it easy for us mere humans, a powerful wizard in a cave in Kentucky called DNS (Domain Name System) takes a name and converts it to the IP address for us. The IP address for my website is 67.15.97.14.

Spyware and viruses often try to send us to sites that we don't want to go to. The window that pops up with the come on to buy Viagra cheap is created by opening a browser window and putting in an address such as www.ripuoff.com which then is converted to a number address and takes us to the site for Viagra. Some

> **Grandma and Grandpa, how come you're so smart?**
> **IP Address:** An identifier for a computer or device on a TCP/IP network.
> I can let a Google's search engine tell me my current IP address by typing My IP in the search box.
> Reasons for knowing our IP address might include tech support, remote desktop connection and more.
> Wrong: I use IP addresses to find public restrooms.

advertising on websites engage in "measuring media metrics" or put another way, they collect information about our browsing, where we have been and what we might be interested in buying.

This is all very interesting but how does that help me? (Martha, he read my mind!) There is one other detail about your computer that can help us. Every computer has an internal address. This address is 127.0.0.1 for all computers, often referred to as the localhost. Additionally, every computer has a little file in it called a HOSTS file. Think of the HOSTS file as a gas station where you stop to get directions to an unfamiliar destination. (No dear, I wasn't lost.) Every time we type an address into our Internet browser like www.someplace.com, our computer first checks with the HOSTS file to see if there is a specific location for that site. If there is no data, then our browser takes us to the website just as it normally would. By default, our computers come with only one entry in the HOSTS file, localhost: 127.0.0.1. (There's no place like home.)

So let's see what would happen if we added www.ripuoff.com 127.0.0.1 to the HOSTS file. If directed to this website, our Internet browser would check the HOSTS file and see that www.ripuoff.com was located at 127.0.0.1 which is our own computer. We know the site isn't on our computer, but the browser is trusting that we would not lie to it, so it looks on our computer for the site and when it doesn't find it, we see the famous "The page cannot be displayed" message. No connection is made to the site and anything malevolent on the website is not transferred to our computer. Hooray! I love this powerful little tool. The HOSTS file on my office PC's contain over ten thousand entries that prevent my computers from connecting intentionally, accidentally or secretively to any of these less than admirable sites. (Yes, my dear niece that is why you couldn't download all that junk on my office computers when you were visiting.) I shouldn't have told you that I had a really crappy Internet connection.) If there is a site that I decide later I do want to visit, I simply edit the HOSTS file; remove the entry for the site and now I can visit that site.

The focus of the HOSTS file has changed from just blocking ads/banners to protecting the computer and the user from the many parasites that roaming the Internet. It doesn't serve much purpose to block the ad banners from displaying as most HOSTS files do, and then get hijacked by a parasite from an evil exploit or download contained on the web site. The object is to surf faster while preserving your Safety, Security and Privacy.

How do we start putting these entries into our HOSTS file? I use one maintained by Mike Burgess at: www.mvps.org/winhelp2002/hosts.htm. Go there, download the HOSTS file and read the directions on where to put the file. Pay particular attention to the special instructions for Vista and Windows 7. Remember the HOSTS file complements your Antivirus and Anti Spyware programs; it is not a substitute for them.

Yes you can get there from here.

SIMPLE SOLUTIONS FOR SIMPLE PROBLEMS

Occam's Razor claims that "simpler explanations are, other things being equal, generally better than more complex ones." This theory is especially apropos to those mystical things our PCs do that often drive us to apoplexy. Our digital domestique do try to give us clues to problems or behaviors that are plaguing us as we try to complete specific tasks. Here are some simple solutions to common tribulations we all seem to run into from time to time.

E-mail seems to be a frequent problem area. Many folks contact me with tales of a recalcitrant e-mail that won't go out. What is the error message I ask? " The command was aborted because the mailbox name is invalid." This error and similar messages indicate an incorrect e-mail address. Users have sworn up and down that the e-mail address is correct, but a careful review generally reveals a missing period, .con instead of .com or a misspelling of the user's name. Make the correction and the e-mail flies off to its destination. Another e-mail complaint is about an e-mail that didn't go but keeps trying to send over and over even though we no longer want it to. Keeping in mind that when we hit the Send button the e-mail goes to a holding folder called the Outbox where it waits until the next connection with our e-mail provider's mail server, usually in a minute or two. The solution here is to open the Outbox, highlight the miscreant e-mail and delete it. Problem solved.

Two more common e-mail error messages seen when using a mail client are: "The connection to the server has failed. Account: 'pop3.something.net', Server: 'pop3.something.net', (something being our Internet mail providers name such as Comcast or Centurylink) Protocol: POP3, Port: 110, Secure (SSL): No, Socket Error: 10061, Error Number: 0x800CCC0E" and "The **server** could not be found." (Account: account name, POPserver:'mail', Error Number: 0x800ccc0d)" The simplest cause for these errors is no Internet connection. The next most common problem is e-mail account settings are incorrect. To eliminate these causes as possibilities, verify that access to the Internet is available by opening a web browser or open a command window and try to ping www.msn.com. If a reply comes back then look at the possibility that the e-mail account is set up incorrectly or something was inadvertently changed.

Another common issue is the call that goes, "I can't get online, it says the "Page cannot be displayed." Generally, this means that we have no connection to the Internet. Several simple steps can usually resolve this

> **Grandma and Grandpa, how come you're so smart?**
> **Server:** Computer designed to process requests and deliver data to other computers over a local network or the Internet.
> Servers can be dedicated to specific tasks such as an e-mail server, a print server or online game servers.
> Websites are hosted on web servers that respond to requests for service from other computers like mine.
> Wrong: The new web server refused to bring coffee and donuts.

issue. Start by looking at the modem and or router. Are all the lights on? If not, check that Fido or Ramunda the cat haven't accidently unplugged the device. If just a few of the lights are on, unplug the modem or router, count to ten and plug it back in. And finally reboot the PC. Remember "Mr. C." Modem, Router, Computer and reboot the devices in that order and test after each reboot to see if Internet connections are active.

Then there is the laptop we use with a wireless router that suddenly won't connect to the Internet. Take a look at the laptop and verify that we haven't accidently turned off the wireless adapter that makes the connection possible. Some laptops have a button on the keyboard, a slide switch on the side of the laptop, a keyboard combination such as FN and F2 that turns the wireless on and off or a program that enables or disables wireless hardware. These are usually accompanied by a blue LED somewhere with a wireless symbol that indicates whether the wireless adapter is on or an orange light to indicate an off state.

A different problem arises when our PC locks up. The mouse freezes, the keyboard doesn't respond even to more than enthusiastic persuasion and nothing we do elicits a response from the digital diva. There is no way to restart the computer. Pushing the power button doesn't seem to get us anywhere and after a few minutes of contemplation we decide to pull the power cord. Those of us with Desktop computers can watch as the computer goes dark. But the folks with laptops often are amazed that nothing happens. Even with the power cord unplugged the laptop stays on. That is because there is a battery in the laptop that allows us to operate for a time away from a power source. To force the laptop to shutdown after pulling the power cord we must also pull the battery. Now both of a laptops power sources are disconnected.

But there might be an even easier way to shut down a frozen computer. Almost all PCs will shut down if we hold the power button in for eight or ten seconds. Then when all the lights go out release the power button and try to restart the computer.

Finally, a frequent question is "where can I read the Bits and Bytes column, I don't get the paper. Sign up for the electronic edition of the Charlotte Sun at http://ee.yoursun.net. For just $3.00 per month not only get access to this column but the Charlotte Sun as well.

UNTANGLE THE TOWER OF BABEL

The Tower of Babel. Everyone knows the story. It is the metaphorical explanation of why there are so many languages in the world. The tale also states that if man were of one language, nothing he tried to do would be impossible. Maybe the construction around the area would go faster and smoother if it were not for the cacophony of different languages being used. Can you read and interpret the following line? El Internet es un lugar asombroso. No? How about this one? Internet ist ein erstaunlicher Platz. No? Neither can I. Unfortunately, there may be morsels of wisdom buried in those words and we would never know. Maybe the old family Bible, with the mysterious writing in it and handed down for generations contain the directions to your family's fortune. A king's ransom smuggled out of some country and hidden in another part of the world just before an invasion of your ancestral home. Or perhaps the letters written to your grandfather from the girl in Italy during World War Two would be interesting and poignant if they could be deciphered.

In my own case, I received a letter from Queen Beatrix of the Netherlands in response to an inquiry sent to her. Probably some Under Assistant Deputy to the Assistant Secretary of Correspondence simply made a mistake but the Queen's letter of reply was in Dutch. Despite my heritage, I don't speak or read Dutch. There it was, a royal letter from the leader of one of the world's most important nations, and I don't know what it says. I was panic-stricken. There was always the possibility that the Queen was going to appoint me burgemeester (Mayor) of my ancestral hometown of Outdorp. (Ok, maybe not a big chance, but could I take that risk?) What to do? Fortunately, I do have some friends that spend time here in Charlotte County that are Dutch so I thought I will just have them translate the letter for me. Unfortunately, none of them were in town when the envelope with the official stamps and embossing on the front of it arrived.

So there it was, a letter from the Queen of the Netherlands in my hands, probably with an urgent plea to begin some important quest. It was imperative that I know what it said before I slipped on my wooden shoes and went forth for her Majesty, tilting at windmills.

Fortunately, the Tower of Babel has been reduced to a parking lot. It is now possible to understand and communicate with people all around the world. If the need arises to **translate** a document, there is a very

Grandma and Grandpa, how come you're so smart?
Translate: Reproduce a written or spoken text in a different language while retaining the original meaning.
Many Internet search engines can translate text by simply typing in the text and specifying the languages.
After translating the letter from the Queen, it was clear that she would not be visiting our town.
Wrong: When flying, I like to translate on the Red Eye.

powerful tool at our disposal. Simply fire up your computer, connect to the Internet and go to http://babelfish.yahoo.com. At this site there are tools to translate specific words from one language to another. For example, the word columnist, translated to Dutch, is kroniekschrijver. But even more interesting is that you can enter an entire block of text and it will translate the document for you. If it is a short passage that interests you, simply type it in. Another Dutch phrase I like is "hij is zeer interessant". Put that phrase in front of kroniekschrijver and it describes this column. For a longer document, use a scanner to capture the document into your computer then simply copy and paste the text into the translator and behold the mysteries laid bare.

Gene Roddenberry, creator of the Star Trek franchise, had to resolve the question how every alien species the crew ran into spoke perfect English. His answer was a Universal Translator that could instantaneously decipher extraterrestrial languages. The original Star Trek episodes took place in the years 2266 – 2269 and at the time seemed very futuristic. Gene may have been right about the technology but he was off on the time scale by a few hundred years.

Today our computers offer to translate from one language to another. All the major search engines offer a translation service for the amazing fee of zero. We simply take a document or paragraph and either copy/paste or type in the foreign language and it is translated almost instantaneously to our language of choice. Want to read a French newspaper? Right mouse click on the page and choose translate with Bing or Google and the page magically appears in English. Perhaps not perfect but well enough to get the drift. Surf over to translate.google.com, babelfish.yahoo.com or www.microsofttranslator.com/ to see what each offers.

Want to learn how to speak a foreign language? Go to free-translator.imtranslator.net/speech.asp, type in or copy/paste the word or phrase in our native language, specify the language to learn and the website says it back to us in the language we select. Don't forget to turn on the speakers. There are many different translators available if these don't do exactly what is desired.

Even more exciting is speech to speech translators. The iPhone and the Android smart phones have translators that can be downloaded and used much like the Star Trek universal translators. Let's use the Android phone as our example but the iPhone has similar features. Download an "app" to the phone, in this example Google's Translate. This small program will allow us to speak, for example English, and translate the words to our language of choice. Traveling to Italy? Want to find a restaurant? Turn on Google Translate, set the language for English to Italian, speak the question, the app translates, touch the speaker and the phone will ask our question in Italian. Or set the phone to translate from Italian to English, allow the waiter to speak to the phone and then read or listen to what was said in English. Another great app for our smart phones is called Google Voice Search or Siri for the new iPhones. This Google app allows us to talk to our smart phones and verbally send text messages, take notes, call people in our contact list, send e-mails, play music, and many other functions.

Thanks Mr. Roddenberry, language is not a barrier anymore.

So for now, Vriendelike Groete. (What did he say, Martha?) Look it up, just like I did.

I FEEL THE NEED FOR SPEED

I feel the need for speed. I recently spent a weekend at Old Town, in Kissimmee FL. Old Town is exactly that, an old section of the town that has been changed to a tourist area, complete with restaurants, bands, and most interesting to me, on Saturday night the town streets are only open to classic cars. But, Old Town also has some amusement rides one of which is two Mustangs on a track. You can drag race your friends to see who has the quicker reaction time off the starting line. The excitement comes though when they hand you your time ticket for the run. In my case, it was elapsed time, two seconds, speed clocked at 109 mph. Zero to 109 mph in two seconds. Unbelievable.

There was a time when computer connections to the Internet were made using a dial up phone line and a 300-baud modem. A baud is a measurement of the number of signaling elements (bits) that occur each second. The term is named after J.M.E. Baudot, the inventor of the Baudot telegraph code. A 300-baud modem transfers 300 bits per second or 300 bps. Different types of modems were developed that allowed multiple bits of information to be passed at the same time, which ultimately brought us where we are today with 56 kbps or 56000 bits per second. Remember, that this rating is the theoretical maximum of the modem. The actual speed is dependant on many things, not least of all being the condition of the phone line. Your modem is most assuredly going to pass data at some speed lower than 56 kbps.

Most dial up internet providers offer some type of "accelerator" for only a small additional fee per month, but if the theoretical maximum is 56 kbps how can they promote "Up to five times faster?" Can their programmers outsmart the laws of the phone company? The truth leans more towards magic. (Martha, he's got something up his sleeve.) Magic is based, not on the supernatural, but on misdirection. And in a manner of speaking, that is what the "accelerator" does.

All accelerators use **file compression**. They take a file that is called for from the Internet and compress the file to a much smaller size. This means it takes less time to appear on your computer. It is still downloaded at 56kbps or less but since much smaller files are downloaded it didn't take as much time. But even the "five times

Grandma and Grandpa, how come you're so smart?
File Compression: Storing data in a format that requires less space than usual.
When emailing very large files, compression to a smaller size lets them upload or download faster.
Backup programs use file compression to take large amounts of data and fit it on smaller storage drives.
Wrong: I wish my diet could be based on file compression rather than proper eating.

faster" is a bit like the theoretical limit. It would be nice but probably unreachable because not all files can be compressed. There are two types of compression used by the accelerators. Files such as text files or html files, which need to be identical to the original when they get to your PC use lossless compression. A typical text file can be compressed up to fifty percent and then reassembled when it is displayed on your PC. On the other hand, pictures use lossy compression. For example, take a picture that originally was made up of 2 million colors. After lossy compression it may only have 16 thousand. There may be a loss in quality but it will appear on your screen much faster because you didn't receive the entire picture.

There are files out there that absolutely cannot be compressed. Things like streaming video, (certainly wouldn't want to miss the good parts) MP3 music files, and any secure sites, such as banks, shopping carts etc that use encryption. So these types of files are going to download to from the Internet at their normal pace.

I feel the need for speed. So how does dial up compare to DSL (Digital Subscriber Line) and Cable Internet providers? Remember dial up transfers data at something less than 56 kbps. DSL on the other hand using traditional copper phone lines, but at different frequencies than voice communication can move data (depending on the service selected) from 785 kbps up to 25 mbps (if available in your area) or million bits per second. Once again this is a theoretical speed because DSL is distance limited. The further your computer is from the phone company's central office the slower the connection will be.

I feel the need for more speed. A cable connection is by far the fastest connection available. As I write this column, my cable connection is downloading data at 12 mbps. If I choose a different package I can get up to 25 mbps 214 times the absolute best possible speed of a dial up connection. So just how fast is your Internet connection?

Go to www.testmy.net, www.speakeasy.net/speedtest or www.dslreports.com and run the download and upload tests. These sites give the speed of your Internet connection using different criteria, compares it to the other forms of connection and weighs it against the average transfer rate for your Internet Service Provider. These sites work for dial up, DSL, Cable, Satellite and ISDN connections.

Just call me Speedy.

WHAT'S THE VALUE OF A BROWSER'S REAL ESTATE?

Real Estate. Here in Charlotte County we know the meaning of Real Estate. Go to a cocktail party and before long the talk invariable turns to Real Estate. "My neighbor bought a twelve hundred foot fixer upper for X dollars and sold it four weeks later for X+. I know a guy that bought a dog house for Z dollars and sold it for the ransom of King Siam a week later. Our neighbors bought a canal property last year for YY and had to sell it this year for –y. Real Estate has produced or reduced more millionaires in this century than any other product. The book "The Millionaire Next Door" by Thomas J. Stanley suggests that you may be living next door to a millionaire and not even be aware of it. (Martha, bring the neighbor some brownies.)

Real Estate however comes in a variety of forms. Grocery stores for example refer to real estate as the shelf space dedicated to a particular product. I.E. a cereal maker such as General Mills desperately tries to control "Real Estate" as it pertains to shelf space dedicated to General Mills cereals in a grocery store.

Lately there seems to be a similar battle in **cyberspace**. Toolbars have become the "undiscovered country" as it pertains to controlling the "Real Estate" on your computer's desktop. For example I recently visited a client that was having some problems accessing the internet. I opened a browser window using Internet Explorer and there, under the buttons at the top of the screen, were a Google toolbar, a Yahoo toolbar, a Bing toolbar, a Sidebar toolbar, and a Nextag toolbar, each one securing a vital piece of the browsers "Real Estate" and leaving an ever smaller browser window with which to view web pages.

Let's review some of the features toolbars offer and what they mean to us. One feature that seems to attract users is the popup blocker feature. Toolbars purport to block unwanted pop ups which we agree is a good thing. However, Internet Explorer 8 and 9 have a very effective pop up stopper built in so the toolbar pop up blocker becomes redundant. But consider, if the PC is plagued by pop ups, then the PC is probably infested with spyware and removing these rogue programs will also eliminate pop ups.

Next let's consider the search capabilities of the toolbars. Google, Yahoo and Dogpile, among others, allow you to search for keywords across the web and even keywords within a specific webpage that is currently displayed. There is some advantage here, especially for someone that spends a lot of time researching points

> **Grandma and Grandpa, how come you're so smart?**
> **Cyberspace:** A virtual universe of electronic data with computers as the ingress and egress points.
> When an e-mail I sent doesn't get to the person I sent it to, it must be floating around in cyberspace.
> Playing games in cyberspace allows for fantastic virtual realities to exist.
> Wrong: A great idea for a new TV show might be Lost in Cyberspace.

and information. Other toolbars use their search capabilities to direct a search to their advertisers which may or may not have a bearing on what we are searching for. There is also the Windows Search bar that resides at the bottom of the screen just above the Start Button (Vista and Windows 7) and doesn't require a browser to be open. Type a keyword search in here and the results of the search are displayed in the start menu. From there a browser window can be opened and the results reviewed.

On the other hand it is also possible to type keywords into a browser's (such as Internet Explorer or Firefox) URL address bar and a search will also be completed. Within the browser window under the menu labeled Edit, is a function called Find which will also search a webpage for specific keywords. So again, while a toolbar may be convenient, this feature is also redundant. While we can applaud convenience, is it sufficiently advantageous to out weigh the loss of "Real Estate" on our browser and adding another program to the list of items using resources on our PC? You'll have to decide.

Toolbars also purport to stop spyware and spam. This is accomplished by running an anti-spyware scan of your computer. For example, Yahoo contracts with Pest Control to provide this service. This is a good feature and Pest Patrol is a well recognized company. But again, Microsoft provides, free of charge for the moment, their Windows Defender program that accomplishes the same thing without stealing "Real Estate" on your browser window. Windows Defender is available to download to Windows XP and is included with Vista and Windows 7.

Is there a downside to the toolbars besides taking over your browsers viewing area? Google is very upfront about the information they collect via their toolbar. This information can be found at http://www.google.com/toolbar/privacy.html. Yahoo also clearly outlines their privacy policy at http://privacy.yahoo.com/privacy/us/toolbar/details.html. Before downloading and installing a toolbar it might be a good idea to read these policies and see if you agree with their goals and objectives.

Other toolbars have other agendas. For example the Comcast toolbar provides many of the same features as Google and Yahoo, but also provides many more ways to link to Comcast controlled content. Not a bad thing if you like Comcast and its services. However there are several so called "Shopping" toolbars that promise that no matter what you search for they will find a site affiliated with them that will sell you something. Wonderful if searching for a new car etc. but if looking for research material, it would be a bit undesirable. Can it be associated with spyware/malware? If you agreed to download it and understood its function, maybe not.

Another drawback to having multiple toolbars on the browser is degradation of the browsers performance. Each toolbar tries to alter the way the browser operates. Many toolbars are benign by themselves but when competing with other toolbars can eventually cause the browser to crash, not open or not respond. Windows even offers a method of resetting the browser to its original state in order to resolve these issues. One of the things this method does is disable all toolbars. To reset an Internet explorer, go to the Control Panel – Internet Options. Click on the Advanced tab and near the bottom click on the button labeled Reset.

Using Firefox? At the top of the Firefox window, click the Firefox button, go over to the Help menu and select Restart with Add-ons Disabled. Firefox will start up with the Firefox Safe Mode dialog. For Windows XP, click the Help menu and select Restart with Add-ons Disabled. If Firefox will not start, hold down the shift key and then start Firefox in safe mode.

Personally, I don't use any toolbars. All the functions of the toolbars are available in my browser and I really don't need any squatters on my Internet browser.

SOMETIMES IT'S BETTER TO SAY NO THAN YES

Remember the time when a salesperson would make their pitch with the hope of convincing us their product was too good to pass by? Recall the days of yesteryear, when we were regaled with the benefits and endless joy we would derive from the purchase of some new wonder product? If our careers were in sales we had the maxim that a mark, I mean potential customer needed to say no five times before we said goodbye. Purchased a new car lately? The sales person works so hard some of them sweat to get you to sign on the dated line and if that doesn't work, it's off to the Sales Manager who bemoans the loss the dealership will take if you grab this deal and what will it take to get you into a car today? Those were the days when even if the sales person swayed us to sign, WE picked up the pen and marked our John Henry on the dotted line. It was our choice.

Alas it appears those days have faded into history. There seems to be a new sale's maxim that is predicated on the premise that we have bought if we don't say no. Even if we didn't realize we were receiving a product, by not responding in the negative we purchased it. This new sales technique is growing more prevalent through out the economy and many examples can be found. Not too long ago, I started getting billed for texting on my cell phone. I called and asked that the charge be removed. I was told that I asked for the service because they gave me thirty days free texting as a courtesy to me, and I didn't cancel it at the end of thirty days. The only problem was they never notified me of the free thirty days, they simply added it to my service plan. There was no way to cancel what I didn't know about so supposedly I bought it. A few conversations with the provider soon brought light to their eyes and they canceled the service.

Our computers are suffering from the same new sales practice. One area that is under severe attack is the browser program. Most of us use Internet Explorer, Firefox, Chrome or Safari. Go ahead and open the browser and look near the top of the **window**. How many toolbars are showing there? A recent problem a client experienced was that Internet Explorer would not open. They clicked on it and it would flash open then close. Looking for a cause took me to Manage Add-Ons. This showed a total of five toolbars trying to modify and control the way Internet Explorer operated. Internet Explorer had thrown up its data bits and keeled over dead. This poor browser was trying to operate with a Google Toolbar, Yahoo Toolbar, Alot toolbar, IWin

> **Grandma and Grandpa, how come you're so smart?**
> **Window:** A rectangular frame on a computer screen in which images output by programs can be displayed, moved around, or resized.
> When I double click on my word program a window opens in which I can type a letter.
> Sometimes a website will try to open a window without my knowledge and my pop up blocker stops it.
> Wrong: There are a few times when I want to throw my computer out the window.

toolbar and an ASK toolbar. All of these are third party programs that alter the way the browser responds to search requests, homepages, cookies and other functions.

How did they get there? Everyone tells me that THEY didn't put them there. And yet they magically appear. They installed not because we asked for them, but because we didn't respond negatively to the acceptance of their installation. A great example that almost everyone has experienced is the Java updates that occasionally ask to be installed. We really do want Java and most of us click the Next button, and the Next button and the Next button and the Finish button. What we miss is a little check box already checked that informs us that the BING toolbar will be installed. If we don't uncheck the box, Bingo, another toolbar. Folks like WeatherBug, but don't UNCHECK the box that says install the weather toolbar, like a bolt of lightning there is the Weather toolbar. Try to install Adobe Reader, did you notice the checkbox already filled in that results in a Google toolbar installed. Download some of the free games so easy to get and low and behold the Delio toolbar appears. Pretty soon we have only a few inches of screen to see the webpage and lots of toolbars that all conflict with each other. It won't be long and the browser will give up and go home.

What can we do? In the future, downloading from the Internet, or installing anything from a disk, look at each page and see if there is something that will be installed unless we remove a checkmark. If it's wanted leave the check in, if not remove it. But what if we miss the checkbox and another toolbar is installed? Open the Control Panel, then Add/Remove Programs (XP) Programs and Features (Vista) Programs (Win7) and look down the list of installed programs. Anything that says toolbar remove it if it is not desired. The browser will thank you.

What if our browser stops working because of add-ons that have choked it off? Internet Explorer 8 has a reset button that disables all toolbars and returns the browser to factory default settings. Open Control Panel, Internet Options, Advanced tab and towards the bottom of the box is a button labeled reset. If using Firefox, go to the Start Button, All Programs, Mozilla then Mozilla Firefox Safe Mode. When it starts a dialogue box appears and two choices are Reset Toolbars and Controls or Reset All User Preferences to Firefox Defaults. Pick one and Firefox will take the appropriate action to free itself from the yoke the add-ons imposed.

Just say no to yes.

NOT ALL WEB BROWSERS ARE CREATED EQUAL

Technological advances move so fast that sometimes we miss the transition from old to new. A good example is the web browser we use to surf the Internet. A web browser is like our TV. It takes the digital signals coming from the Internet and converts them into a graphical user interface on the monitor. It allows us to print, scroll, link to, watch movies and many other features that we find helpful. The first web browsers appeared approximately 1993 and most web information contained only text. Over time, programmers began to incorporate pictures, games and videos, enriching our surfing experience. The top three browsers by market share are Internet Explorer, Firefox and Chrome. Programmers continue to improve speed, visual appearance and protections against viruses and phishing attacks with each new release.

On the other side of the equation are the websites we visit. Each site must be programmed to display properly in different browsers. They must also display properly in different versions of the same the browser. An example of this is the differences between Internet Explorer 8 which is the latest version that can be run on Windows XP and Internet Explorer 9 which is the version shipped with new Windows 7 PCs. Sometimes websites don't get updated right away to the newest version and strange things appear when displayed in Internet Explorer 9. For example, parts of a webpage might be missing, information in a table might be in the wrong locations, or colors and text might be incorrect. Some web pages might not display at all. If using IE9 there are steps we can take to resolve these issues.

If IE9 identifies a site that isn't compatible it will display the Compatibility View button on the URL **Address bar**. The address bar has the www.something.com name of the site we are visiting. The Compatibility View button resembles a piece of paper with a tear running across it. To turn Compatibility View on, click the Compatibility View button to make the icon change from an outline to a solid color. The site will then be displayed as if we were using an earlier version of Internet Explorer. IE9 will also remember that the site needs the Compatibility View in the future and will always display it properly when we return.

Firefox uses plug-ins and Chrome has an extension that can be downloaded and installed to enable it to

---

Grandma and Grandpa, how come you're so smart?
Address bar: A text field near the top of a Web browser window that displays the URL of the current webpage.
If I know the web address of a site I can type the www.something.com in the address bar to save time.
The browser's address bar will also turn different colors if the site has security issues.
Wrong: A great name for a nightclub would be the Address Bar.

display sites that will only work in Internet Explorer.

Another feature in Internet Explorer is the Tracking Protection feature. Tracking Protection prevents websites from tracking our online activity. It can be turned off for a single website if it's blocking content we want see. To turn Tracking Protection on or off, open IE9 and click on the tool at the top that looks like a gear. From the dropdown menu click on Safety and click on Tracking Protection and enable it. From the address bar we can also disable Tracking Protection for a single site if it is preventing the site from displaying content we wish to see.

SEARCH ENGINES CAN BE HELPFUL

Do any of us really know the amazing things that we can do just by typing a few keystrokes? How many folks have experimented with search engines? Is it possible that search engines such as Google, Bing and many others have some unique features that might amuse, amaze and enlighten? Strap in for a quick tour of some interesting search engine features.

Fire up Google (www.google.com) and type in any land line phone number. Google will do a reverse lookup and display the name of the owner. There are other sites that will also provide this information such as www.anywho.com all for the amazing price of FREE. (Martha, that's a great price.)

Google will look up shipment tracking numbers and even airline schedules by simply typing in the tracking numbers or flight number such as United Flight 1223. This can save us the chore of having to log in to the website and navigate to the information we want. Google has incorporated into its search engine Google Suggests. This is an **algorithm** that compares what we type as we type it into the search box with other search keywords. Google explains it this way. "Google's auto complete algorithm offers searches that might be similar to the one you're typing. Start to type [new york] -- even just [new y] -- and you may be able to pick searches for "New York City," "New York Times," and "New York University" (to name just a few)."Typing in a long string? Google may suggest what we want before we finish typing. Simply click on the suggestion to have the search engine take us there.

Google offers some other very simple features with their search engine that can come in handy. Type "time Portland, Or, and Google will display the time in Portland. Type weather Miami, FL, Google displays the weather. Want news for our old hometown, type news Lancaster, Pa and up it pops. Remember capitalization is not necessary to make this work. Same thing works for stock quotes, just type in the ticker symbol and the latest stock information is available. Want to see the latest news about an earthquake? To see information about recent earthquakes in a specific area type "earthquake" followed by the city and state or U.S. zip code. For recent earthquake activity around the world simply type "earthquake" in the search box. Google offers

> **Grandma and Grandpa, how come you're so smart?**
> **Algorithm:** A formula or set of steps for solving a particular problem.
> Baking a cake involves a type of algorithm called a recipe.
> There are many routes I could take to work and they represent different solution paths or algorithms.
> Wrong: Concepts about climate change will eventually be referred to as algorithms.

many more search engine tricks. Surf over www.google.com/help/features.html to see a list of the features available, explanations and examples.

Bing is search engine available from Microsoft and it too has some helpful tricks. Bing will also do conversions right from the search field. Want to know how many teaspoons in a cup, type in cup = teaspoons and Bing will deliver the answer of forty eight. Looking for word definitions? Type define: Stertor and Bing will display the meaning of the word. Bing is so confident that users will prefer search results as presented by Bing, even if we like and use the iGoogle home page, they have created a Firefox add-in to redirect a search typed into the Google search box to Bing for execution. If using Firefox as our Internet browser download and install the gBing add in to use this app.

Both Google, Bing and most search engines allow us to search by image instead of text in response to our query. Open our search engine of choice, click on the tab labeled Images and start our search. Pictures that relate to our search will appear. In addition to displaying pictures in response to our query, the ability to sort these images by size is a click of the mouse.

Just for fun surf over to the Internet Archive (www.archive.org/) which is a search engine that has been taking snapshots of the entire World Wide Web for years now, allowing us to travel back in time to see what a web page looked like in 1999, or what the news was like around Hurricane Katrina in 2005. I have used Yahoo since their inception and I was able to see what the website looked like then. Ah memories.

There are many other search engines, hundreds in fact. Type "top search engines" into any search field to see a list of companies that serve up Internet results to our burning questions. Each engine may display different results and one may be more relevant than another. The world's knowledge is at our fingertips.

What do you want to know today?

YIKES, I CAN'T OPEN THIS FILE!

The Punta Gorda Block Party is fast approaching. We will see a sea of singing, a plethora of people and even blocks of booths with things to taste, buy or look at. I enjoy the block party because there are often things there that mean nothing to me because I don't know what they are. For example, my first look at swamp cabbage, what in the world was it and why would anyone go get it, cook it and then eat it?

Sometimes we all see things that we cannot understand or interpret with the tools and experiences we have gained in our lives. If these things are important to us, we will get some education or acquire some new equipment or seek help in gaining comprehension of the mystery before us.

Our computers are similar. They can show us fascinating new pictures, or documents but only if they know how to clarify the data. If not, then we get a red X or the message, "there is no program associated with this file." Or put another way, if we needed to remove a screw from a piece of wood and all we had was a hammer, we couldn't do the job.

Almost everyone has a computer or access to one. But there the similarity starts to break down. There are many different programs for modifying pictures, creating emails, spreadsheets, databases etc. Each program creates a file with a certain footprint. To clarify, imagine going to the beach and looking at all the footprints in the sand. All the prints were made by a human, but each footprint belongs to a specific human. Computer programs are just like that. Documents are all made by word processing programs, but each document belongs to a specific program and often can only be opened and used by that particular program.

How can we identify which program was used to create the file we want to see? That **extension** after each file name is the clue. If we see a ".doc" then we know the document was made by MS Word. If it has an ".xls" at the end it is a spreadsheet made by MS Excel. Another example is ".pdf" which is a file generated in Adobe PDFwriter.

Grandma and Grandpa, how come you're so smart?
Extension: A set of characters following the period after the name of a file, identifying the file type. Every program has its own file extension for the type of file it creates for example PDF or DOC. The extension after a file's name tells the computer which program is needed to open that file.
Wrong: I asked my computer for a loan extension.

Clients call and say they received a file via email from a friend but when they try to open it, they get a message that there is no program associated with that file. This simply means that the computer has no program that will open and display the file they received. How do we correct that?

Let's look at one of the more common examples out there today. Many people use MS Office to create documents, presentations, databases, spreadsheets etc. These are great tools and can generate very interesting items. However, if the person receiving the file does not have MS Office, there is a very real probability that they will not be able to open and view the file. All the hard work that went into creating the item will be wasted. What can be done? We could go out and buy MS Office, install it and no more problems. Except that MS Office starts around $200 and may be a bit pricy for some folks. There is an alternative.

Microsoft has recognized that not everyone will run out and buy their product, but realizes that for the people that do, they need to be able to send files created in MS Office that others can see. To this end they have created a series of "viewers" that will allow us to see the documents. We cannot use the viewers to create, change or modify the files, but we can display them. Microsoft makes these viewers FREE to anyone that wants to download and install them. (Martha, I love the sound of that word.) Here is a list of viewers available from Microsoft and Adobe.

PowerPoint Viewer opens presentation files with the extension .pps or .ppt
Word Viewer opens text document files with the extension .doc
Excel Viewer opens spreadsheet files with the extension .xls
Adobe Reader allows us to open files with the extension .pdf

All these programs are free to download and use. The Powerpoint, Word and Excel viewers are available by surfing over to http://www.microsoft.com/downloads/. Once there use the search field and type in viewers to get a list of the programs above, download and install them to your computer. They will open automatically the next time a file is opened with the corresponding file extension.

Surf on over to www.adobe.com and click on Adobe Reader to download the latest version of the program which will allow us to open and read .pdf files.

But what if the file we are trying to open is not one of the common ones that most of us see? There are thousands of different file extensions most of which we will never see or use. Should we come across a file that defies our attempts to open it, and it is not one of the extensions listed in this column, surf over to www.file-extensions.org/extensions/common where we find a list of file extensions that will choke a horse. For example; someone emails us a file with the extension MPEG-4. This site will explain that the file is an audio file and will list a few of the programs that will play this file. Sometimes a program can be had just for downloading it. Specialized file extensions may require the purchase of the program that created the file.

We can also put the file extension such as .html in a search engine and within a few moments we will have lots of websites that will tell us what the file is and which program will open it.

I can see clearly now.

HOW TO POOF YOU'RE RIGHTING WIT GRATE CARE

Some of you are going to find this hard to believe. There are weeks when I struggle to put together a column that is interesting, educational and humorous. The computer and Internet always offers some interesting items. There is always something we can learn and Charlotte County can provide all the humor we can stand. (Conserve water, let's build 3200 homes in Murdock, approve those 7000 residences and endorse the ordinance requiring us to shower with a friend.)

With these three prerequisites I can still struggle for days to scribe a tome that is easy to understand, fun to read and best of all folks say "I learned something today." My biggest fear is that my most vociferous critic will read it and say "Honey, this is not very good."

To save time I use MS Word to write out my columns each week. My editor provides me with an abbreviated and tailored version of the Associated Press Style guide that sets standard ways to present things like abbreviations, quotes, word usage, capitalization and other features common to newspaper columns. MS Word has the ability to accept many of these style guides as tools so that if writing in a hurry to meet a deadline, MS Word will automatically correct items that do not meet the requirements of the Style Guide.

For example: The guide says that the word "Internet" must always be capitalized. I can tell MS Word that every time I type "internet" it should automatically capitalize it whether I did or not. MS Word will also correct spelling for us. It already knows that if we type "teh" or "mroe" by mistake, it will replace it with "the" or "more" automatically. MS Word has a dictionary built in that compares what we type to the dictionary and corrects it if necessary or offers us a choice of spellings if there are multiply entries. It also has the capability to **import** additional dictionaries if our writing needs the support of a technical lexicon or even a foreign language vocabulary.

This is especially useful for words that we type by habit but really want a different word or even words to appear. We can open MS Word, click on Tools, then AutoCorrect Options and type the word we want to

> **Grandma and Grandpa, how come you're so smart?**
> **Import:** To transfer data from one program to another, especially when a change of format is required.
> Having finished the spreadsheet of customers, it was time to import it into a label making program.
> The Windows Live Photo Gallery program will import pictures from my camera to the computer.
> Wrong: Many kudos go out to very import Aunt Martha.

always change in the field labeled "Replace". Next to it is a field labeled "With" and here we can type the word or phrase that should always be substituted for the word we don't want. Example: If I type the word "wife" MS Word will always replace it with "the one I love." (Why use one word when four will do?) This feature can be very helpful to those that write letters to the editors. Write the way you feel (you %#$@* no good &^%$#) and if MS Word is set up correctly, it will come out "Dear Commissioner whose only concern is my well being."

Another great tool for those of us that have the latest version of MS Word has to do with the ability to set the program to save documents in other formats. Not all our friends have the newest version of Word and if we save it in the default new version and send it to them they may not be able to open and read it. Go to Tools – Options and click on the Save tab. There is a pull down labeled "Default Format." Click on the pull down and change the default format to "Word 97-2003 & 6.0\95 – RTF.doc." Now the document can be opened and read in all versions of Word.

Other useful features to be found in MS Word under Tools are the ability to track changes. This tool identifies every change made to a document and notes it in the margins. When several people are reviewing a document and making modifications to it, this tool makes it easy for everyone to see what was added or deleted without going back to an original document and scanning for changes. I recently was asked to review a letter to a major auto manufacturer and used "Track Changes" so the modifications I made to the document were apparent to the author and he could accept or reject them if he chose.

Finally a cautionary note. MS Word is not smart. It simply compares words to dictionaries and sentence construction to standard norms. If we use the wrong word but spell it properly, MS Word will not correct us.

So remembrance to poof you're righting wit grate care. The arrows maid wilt be yarns.

FILE CONVERTERS CAN HELP

Progress marches on. Many of us are purchasing new computers and new software to go with it. We like to keep on the leading edge rather than the bleeding edge. One software package that many users are adding to the arsenal of tools available to them is Microsoft Office 2010 with its Word, Excel and other components. These programs are useful, full of features and make our daily chores easier. We can send out that newsletter, weekly bulletin, letters and even holiday cards.

But across the land we hear from the recipients of our missives, "I can't open the attachment." Investigation reveals that there are many more users still chugging away on Office 2000, XP or 2003. Starting with Office 2007 Microsoft changed the default file format for documents from .doc to .docx, spreadsheets from .xls to .xlsx and PowerPoint files from .pps to .ppsx which are not compatible with the older versions and hence cannot be opened. Do not despair; there are some options available to remedy this dilemma.

One alternative is to notify the sender that we cannot open the file in its current format and would they resave the document in an older format. Using a Word document as our example (the process is the same for Excel and PowerPoint) start Word 2007 or 2010, open the document to be converted from ".docx" to an earlier format. Click the "Office" button in the upper left corner of the screen. Move the pointer to "Save As" and a side menu will pop out. Select the option for "Word 97-2003." This will save the file in .doc **format**.

They can also have Word 2007 or 2010 save by default to ".doc" instead of ".docx." This is accomplished by opening Word, clicking on the "Office" button in the top left corner. Next click the "Word Options" button. Select "Save" from the options bar on the left, and select "Word 97-2003" from the "Save files in this format" drop down section. Click "OK." Now our files will save as ".doc" by default.

Perhaps a more efficient method for users still utilizing older versions of Office is to surf over to www.microsoft.com/download. In the search box labeled Search Download Center type in Office Compatibility Pack for Word. Download the Microsoft Office Compatibility Pack for Word, Excel and

Grandma and Grandpa, how come you're so smart?
Format: The structure or organization of digital data for storing, printing, or displaying.
The most common use of format refers to a word document and how it is laid out.
Format is also used to define the type of file we are working with such as a word document or spreadsheet.
Wrong: Mathew looked out over the adoring crowd and knew the love was all format.

PowerPoint File Formats and follow the steps to install it on the computer. Remember this is for older versions of Office and is not needed if running Office 2007 or 2010. This download is a file converter that will allow older versions of Office to open, edit and save the .docx formats as if they were .doc files.

For those of us still using Microsoft Works Word Processor or Works Spreadsheet this converter also allows Works to open .docx files however some of the font, paragraph and other special formatting features may be lost or modified to allow the file to open in Works.

While the downloaded file converter is an easy way to extend the capabilities of our software, the software itself, old or new has many converters already built into it. Again using Word as the example, if we click on File then Open and browse through the folder where our documents reside we will see a list of all the files there that have the default format. Older versions will list document ending in .doc and new versions will display documents suffixed with .docx. But if we look at the bottom of the dialogue box we will see a dropdown box labeled Files of Type. If we click on the pull down arrow a list of formats that Word has the capability of opening. Even files created in other company's formats such as WordPerfect can be converted and opened by Word. If the file we are looking for still doesn't appear there we can change the File of Type to (All Files.) This may let us see the file we want in the list but doesn't guarantee it can be opened.

From this dropdown we also have the ability to take a document and convert it and save it to any of the formats listed there. So if we know that the person to which the document will be sent does not have Word, WordPerfect some other productivity suite, we can save it in .txt or .rtf which can be opened in Notepad if necessary.

And don't forget, if we don't have Office or WordPerfect and finances are an issue, surf over to www.openoffice.org and download the latest version of OpenOffice. This is a fully capable productivity suite that can open and edit .docx, .xlsx and .ppsx files and save as .doc, .xls and .pps files.

Nobody has to know we live on the bleeding edge.

TIP TOE THROUGH THE TOOLTIPS

The beginning of July and one of my New Year resolutions is still unbroken. At the beginning of the year I resolved to expand my office. While it may be a bit easier to get permitting and financing now to build a new office, it is still easier to take advantage of the existing space available. So I decided to expand my office to all of Charlotte County. Imagine a multiple hundred square mile office. All I need is an Internet connection to the World Wide Web, some good victuals and something to quench my thirst. So this week I decided to plop down in a corner of my new office that offered good food, a beverage to match and a wireless connection to the Internet as well.

Choosing a lunch item from the menu was the toughest part of the day. Lot's of choices but think how difficult it would have been with out the menus. Walk into a restaurant and play twenty questions with the server. Do you have sandwiches? Do you have chicken sandwiches? What beverages do you serve? It might take all day to figure out what the restaurant served before we could even order. Think of the menu as a food tip.

Sometimes our computers can seem equally overwhelming when trying to figure out what button on the screen does what. Time and experience can make selection of the correct button fast and easy. When I am working on a PC a client will comment that I click buttons and open and close windows faster than they can figure out what each one was. That is experience. But for the novice there is a very simple tool built into the Windows operating system to help us navigate around. That same tool is an industry standard and is used by nearly every software company when they write new software such as a word processor or even a game. This tool is called a **ToolTip**.

The ToolTip is a common GUI (graphical user interface) element. It activates by hovering the mouse pointer over a button on a tool bar or over a link or picture on a web page. When activated, a small box appears displaying supplementary information regarding the item being hovered over. Let's try it out. Hold the mouse pointer over the time in the system tray. See the box that pops up with the day, date and year? That is a tooltip.

Grandma and Grandpa, how come you're so smart?
  ToolTip: A small pop-up window displaying a brief description of a toolbar button when a computer mouse hovers over that button.
I can use the mouse to hover a cursor over a button and a ToolTip appears to describe available functions.
Tooltips are a small text box with a yellow background and appear if we roll the mouse over a button.
Wrong: Life isn't a tiptoe through the ToolTips.

Open Internet Explorer move the mouse over one of the icons in the toolbar. After a moment or so, a little box appears telling us what that button does. For example: I move the cursor over the icon of the envelope and a box pops up that tells me that if I click on this button I will read mail. Now move the mouse over the START button and let it hover there for a moment. See the box that pops up and tells you "Click here to begin?" That is a ToolTip. Now open your favorite word processor program and move the mouse pointer over one of the many icons on the toolbars. After a moment a box pops up and tells you what it does. Check Spelling, Copy or Paste and Justify are just a few of the ToolTips that I can find in MS Word.

Another valuable tool that many people don't utilize is the ability to open multiple windows and programs at the same time. Right now I have MS Word open as I write this column; I have Internet Explorer open as I research different topics. I have Windows Live Mail open so I can read and send mail and I also have Notepad open for a place to hold partial thoughts and sentences that I don't like but am not ready to delete. But how can I see the windows that are open behind the one I am working in?

Look at the three boxes in the upper right-hand corner of the window's title bar. Click on the first square, marked with a line on the bottom, to minimize the window. The window then disappears from your screen, but its icon is visible on your taskbar. Now hold the mouse pointer over the icon on the taskbar and a ToolTip appears telling us what program the button represents. To open the window again, click on the taskbar icon. Remember that minimizing the window doesn't close the program. The program is still running, using system resources and available for immediate use if we need it.

With apologies to Tiny Tim, let's Tip Toe through the ToolTips.

CREATE LETTERS AND FORMS USING TEMPLATES

Remember the first paint by numbers masterpiece we created? Carefully looking at the numbers that told us which color to use and then which area to paint in. Each area and color separate from the others and yet, when it was all finished, we could step back and see a beautiful landscape, horse or seascape. The canvas (cardboard more likely) with the lines and numbers on it was our template, a guideline for creating our magnum opus. In addition to guiding our brush strokes, the template saved us the time and effort required to sketch the outlines, proportions and depth of scale we required to achieve our work of art.

Local governments also use templates to guide the changes to our area. Zoning rules are templates; MSBUs are a type of template. Once the templates are in place then appropriate growth or progress can fill in to create the desired result, just like our paint by numbers projects, without having to revisit every area for each and every development. This saves us great amounts of time, and provides a consistency to our work.

Many programs on our computers also use **templates**. Let's concentrate on word processing programs. The most common and popular programs that folks use to write letters are Microsoft Works Word Processor, WordPerfect, OpenOffice and Microsoft Word. Works or WordPerfect often come preloaded on a new pc and are useful, utilitarian programs that get the job done for most common tasks. OpenOffice is a full featured word processor and MS Word is a very powerful word processing program that incorporates many more features than the average word processor. It is sometimes bundled on a new machine as a sixty day trial. Regardless of which one you use, there are some great ways to save time by not having to reinvent the wheel.

When you open any word processing program the first thing that you see is a blank sheet. This is a template. It happens to be a template of a blank sheet but it is a template. Works and WordPerfect include many useful templates that are stored on your PC when the program is installed. MS Word has some templates stored on the PC and the program is linked to office.microsoft.com where hundreds if not thousands of templates can be found and downloaded into Word. The charge for these templates? Nada, zip, zero. While I am referencing only word processing documents, the same template availability is there for spreadsheets, greeting cards etc.

Grandma and Grandpa, how come you're so smart?
Templates: A master or pattern from which other similar things can be made
Reinventing the wheel seems pointless when there are so many templates available to use.
Creating a birthday card is easy when we use a card template and just fill in the text.
Wrong: Make sure you wash templates and put them away afterward.

Hundreds of OpenOffice templates can be found at templates.services.openoffice.org which are also very affordable because they are FREE.

Just this morning I needed a letter to cancel my insurance. I opened MS Word, clicked on File – New and Templates. Then in the search field I typed cancellation and fifteen different cancellation letters appeared. Request to Cancel Service, Cancellation of Entire Order, Cancel Subscription and more. I picked one, downloaded it to the word program and then made the appropriate changes that I needed, such as the name of the insurance company, address etc. This saved time because the document was already formatted in a business type letter, contained spaces for pertinent information and the message was clear and concise.

Another client had spent hours trying to create a list that he could use to keep track of all his prescription medicines, which doctors prescribed which medicine, when he needed to refill and the insurance companies that covered which drug. I suggested that he look for a template and sure enough, The Medication Flowsheet template had everything he needed. He downloaded the template and began to fill in the blanks with his personal information.

There are even party invitations that can be downloaded complete with graphics and cute limericks if the need arises for a celebration. And the best part is that these are FREE. MS Works has a more limited selection for download from Microsoft but then most of the Works templates are loaded with the program onto your computer. There are also many other non-Microsoft sites where templates for Works are available, some for free and some for purchase.

Other useful tools with these programs are tutorials that can teach us all the tips and tricks. For WordPerfect take a look at the website etd.vt.edu/howto/tutorials/Word/Word97. For MS Works Word Processor take a look at www.internet4classrooms.com/on-line_works.htm. And finally for MS Word, I have found this site to be very useful, http://www.baycongroup.com/wlesson0..htm. Don't overlook Youtube.com for video presentations on techniques for specific tasks for any of these programs. Surf to Youtube.com and type in the search field the question for the task in question. For example, type Microsoft Works Word processor and a multitude of videos will appear explaining how to perform different functions in the program.

Now I can become a Man of Letters, just like Thomas Jefferson except without the quill and ink.

E-MAIL FOR TECH SUPPORT

Mark Twain said, "There's always a hole in theories somewhere if you look close enough." One theory that computer and software makers believe is that a person in the US and a person in (India, Asia or anywhere for that matter) can converse over a phone and solve a problem. Let's test that theory.

Grab a friend and head into the kitchen. One of you will be the user and the other will be the customer service tech on the other end. Tie a blindfold on the customer service tech and put the tech in the living room. Go into the kitchen and pull out a favorite recipe. Call the tech and say, "I don't know how to make lasagna (or your favorite recipe).

Now have the tech say, "I am happy to help you resolve this issue, I am standing here beside myself with solution for problem." (accent of choice) Try to describe the process of making the recipe.

"I can't find my pan," you say. He says, "I understand your concern, be assured that a resolution of this problem is my goal today. Can you tell me what pan is needed for this process?" "A 9x13 is what it says I should use but I can't open the drawer to get the pan." "I am not sure that there is a 9x13 pan available with this kitchen." And on and on and on.

Here is the hole in the theory. The tech on the phone cannot see what you see, you and he will use different words to describe the same thing, and while he speaks English, it isn't the same language that we use. I once received a call from a client who told me that the modem had died and would I come fix it. Being proactive I grabbed a new **modem** and arrived only to find that the computer was dead. The client thought the computer was called a modem.

There is another way that may lower the frustration level. Never call customer support. All the major computer and software manufacturers offer email or chat support. Email is the best way. Go to the site of the

---

Grandma and Grandpa, how come you're so smart?
Modem: An electronic device that facilitates transmission of data to or from a computer via telephone or other communication lines.
Some folks use a telephone modem while others use a cable or DSL modem to connect to the Internet.
With a modem every PC can be part of the Internet and give access to the entire world's knowledge.
Wrong: Computers are probably one of the crowning achievements of modem times.

company that created the computer or software and look for a link that says contact tech support. Notice I said "the company that created the computer or software." Many times clients tell me they called their Internet provider to solve a problem with their Palm Pilot software, or contacted the computer manufacturer because they couldn't remember their e-mail password and don't understand why the tech couldn't help them.

There you will find an email form that allows you to identify the problem, describe the problem and send it off to someone in their tech support area. Here is the great part about it. They will email you back in ENGLISH with questions to clarify your problem or solutions to try.

Also try to capture any error messages that appear. Telling the tech there is an error means nothing. Telling him the error says "We apologize for this inconvenience, but Windows did not start successfully. A recent hardware or software change might have caused this:" is an error he can lookup and offer solutions for. Ask the tech in the email if there are any event logs that might assist him and if so how to find them and attach them to the email. Also tell them if you have added any new hardware or software recently. Learn how to capture a picture of the screen using Snipping Tool (Vista and Windows 7) or print screen (XP) or even use a digital camera to photograph the error message. Add it to the email so the tech can SEE what happened.

Remember that phone techs are probably not even trained computer techs. They are working from a problem solving book. For example: If you say the computer will not start, they look up that section of the book. Then they have you try the first thing on the list of possible solutions. If that doesn't work then they go to the next. The danger here is that if the information you give to them doesn't make sense, they have no way to know which part of the book to turn to. That is usually when they say, put in the restore disks and return the computer to its original state. Yes, you will lose everything but the computer will work.

Dealing with technical support by e-mail and chat works well, or call a local tech.

REGISTRY CLEANERS - DANGER, DANGER

I was struck with an interesting phenomenon the other day. Riding my bicycle along a section of US41 and because of the amount of traffic, traffic lights and maybe some other issues I couldn't see, I was actually traveling faster than the cars trying to get to their destinations. County and state spend millions of tax dollars on computer controlled lights, intersection control islands, stripes, arrows, signs and driver education only to watch traffic grind ever slower and slower. They even hire more consultants to suggest improvements that ultimately lead to… longer commute times.

Computers are similar to highways. It seems that the longer we have a computer the slower it gets. Like our roads, the obvious answer reminds me of the question about ducks flying south for the winter in the familiar V pattern. . Why is one side of the V longer than the other? Because there are more ducks on that side. Why does traffic move slower? More cars. Why do our computers run slower? More programs.

How can we improve performance? The answer seems self evident. For roads, remove cars. Computers, remove programs. But even this solution poses its own problems. There is an area just north of Veterans Blvd that was platted many years ago. Roads were put in, but nothing else. There is virtually no traffic but it is used to illegally dump, and off-road vehicles tear up the landscape. We could resolve some of the issues by tearing up the roads and returning the area to its natural state. The same plan can be used to clean up our computers by removing unused programs and files. But a magic bullet would be faster, so we hire more consultants for the roads and we download **Registry** cleaners that promise to speed up our computers after only a few minutes and $49.95.

What is the registry? The registry is a system-defined database used by the Windows operating system to store configuration information. More simply, it is a road system that the computer uses to find everything loaded on it and make use of it. It also stores the settings we tell a program to use when we install it. It makes sense that if parts of the road become unusable, or go to dead ends, our computer will slow down as it navigates through the maze.

> **Grandma and Grandpa, how come you're so smart?**
> **Registry:** A hierarchical database storing configuration settings & options on Windows operating systems.
> Every time we add or remove a program from our computer the registry makes changes.
> We can see the registry entries by running regedit32.exe but don't touch if we don't know what it is.
> Wrong: I put a list of gifts I want for my birthday on the registry.

Many folks have downloaded purported registry cleaning programs that promise to instantly remove dead registry entries and thereby speed up our computers. With flashing screens and impressive looking charts they boldly declare our computers are riddled with registry errors. Errors? What they are locating are leftover registry entries that are tied to nothing. Cleaning the unused entries from the registry would at best speed up any search for information within the registry which almost no one does. Oddly, if it were this simple, one wonders why Microsoft, the creators of Windows, does not provide a registry cleaner. They should know the ins and outs of the registry better than anyone. Perhaps a clue comes from Mark Russinovich, Ph.D. Computer Engineering, Microsoft Technical Fellow who states "A few hundred kilobytes of unused keys and values causes no noticeable performance impact on system operation. Even if the registry was massively bloated there would be little impact on the performance of anything other than exhaustive searches."

Registry cleaners, while apparently having no effect on performance, do allow us to perform registry hygiene by cleaning up dead entries. Generally these dead keys and values are created by the removal of programs via the Add/Remove feature in Windows. The problem with the $49 registry cleaners is that they have an automatic feature that most of us use. This automatic feature does not discriminate; it just removes keys and values. To demonstrate the danger of the automatic feature, I recently tested one of the "leading" registry cleaners on my test PC. It ran a scan, found over 400 registry "errors" and then removed them. I restarted the PC and it would not boot up. Apparently some of the registry "errors" were critical to the operation of Windows. The moral here is that if you must use a registry cleaner, find one that can be run in manual mode, has a backup feature that allows the restoration of entries removed from the registry, remove only those entries left from program removal and is FREE or included with a leading antivirus suite.

The MacAfee and Norton Security Suites along with most major antivirus programs provide a registry cleaner under the tools section. Another FREE cleaner can be found at www.ccleaner.com that has a backup mode just in case. Before taking any action regarding the registry be certain that you only change values in the registry that you understand or have been instructed to change by a trusted source. Be sure to back up the registry before making any changes.

Keep that traffic flowing.

RECALIBRATE LAPTOP BATTERIES

Vacations are a wonderful thing. We relax, unwind and clear our minds. For months on end we go to work, work hard during the execution of projects and then get a little down time between the end of the last project and the start of the next. When we finally get a little time off, all we can think of is not doing the very thing we have done day in and day out. A few days later we come back refreshed, sharp and raring to go. We can pick up where we left off, focused, on track and feeling like a new person.

Laptops need a vacation too. Most of us do not take the maintenance steps needed to extend the life of our batteries. There are several things we can do to lengthen the life of the battery. Laptops made in the last few years are equipped with Lithium-Ion batteries. Battery cells suffer gradual, irreversible capacity loss over time. Such aging occurs more rapidly as temperature and discharge loads increase. Here are some suggested ways to minimize the capacity loss for your battery and get the maximum life from them.

We should store Li-Ion batteries between 20°C and 25°C (68°F and 77°F) with 30% to 50% charge. Do not leave batteries exposed to high temperatures for extended periods. Prolonged exposure to heat (for example, inside a hot car) will accelerate the deterioration of Li-Ion cells. Remove the battery if the notebook will be stored (turned off and not plugged into AC power) for more than 2 weeks. Remove the battery if the notebook will be plugged into AC power continuously (via a wall adapter or docking station) for more than 2 weeks.

Every laptop battery has a "fuel gauge" which monitors the battery's state-of-charge. Short discharges and recharges do not fully synchronize the battery's fuel gauge with the battery's state-of-charge. This can result in the amount of power available in one cycle being less than expected or the battery meter being inaccurate. Or more accurately the batteries in our laptops need a chance to relax. Does your laptop seem to die sooner than usual when using the battery? It might be time for a new battery, or it may simply be time to recalibrate the battery. So how can we reset or recalibrate the fuel gauge?

Here are four easy steps for Windows XP machines.

> **Grandma and Grandpa, how come you're so smart?**
> **Laptop:** A personal computer with a screen small and light enough to be operated on the user's lap.
> Generally a laptop is great for people on the go, but more folks are using them as stationary home PCs.
> A laptop usually has a battery that allows for use in out of the way places without access to electricity.
> Wrong: When my knees are cold I throw a quilt over them which I refer to as my laptop.

Step 1 - Disable the Windows Power Management
- In Windows, right-click the Desktop and select Properties in the menu list.
- Click the Screen Saver tab and then click the Power button.
- Under Power schemes, select Always On in the drop down menu.
- Under Settings for Always On power scheme, select Never in each of the drop down menus.
- Click OK on Power Options Properties window, then click OK on the Display Properties window.

Step 2 - Fully charge the battery
- Connect the AC adapter to the notebook.
- Charge the battery until the Windows battery meter is at 100%.

Step 3 - Fully discharge the battery
- Remove the AC adapter.
- Keep the notebook on until the battery has totally drained and the notebook automatically turns off.
- Connect the AC adapter to the notebook.
- Keep the AC adapter connected to the notebook until the battery has completely charged.

Step 4 - Enable the Windows Power Management
- In Windows, right-click the Desktop and select Properties in the menu list.
- Click the Screen Saver tab and then click the Power button.
- Under Power schemes, select Portable/Laptop in the drop down menu.
- Click OK on Power Options Properties window and then click OK on Display Properties window.

Here are the steps for Vista and Windows 7 PCs. Follow the steps below to calibrate the battery power meter readings.

- Connect the AC adapter and allow the battery to charge to 99% - 100% of capacity.
- Disconnect the AC adapter from the notebook PC.
- Click Start , enter power in the Search field, and then select Power Options from the list.
- Select Create a power plan from the left sidebar.
- Click in the Plan name field and type Calibrator . Then, press Enter .
- Select Never for all topics in the On battery column.
- Click Create to accept the values and force the battery to consistently discharge.
- Allow the battery to discharge completely until the notebook PC shuts down.
- NOTE: The battery power meter is now calibrated, and the battery level readings should be accurate.
- Connect the AC adapter and restart the notebook PC.
- After calibration, return to the Power Options dialog box (Step 3) and select a default power plan setting.

After completing the steps above, your notebook PC battery will be calibrated and the battery meter will display the correct state-of-charge.

What did you do on your vacation?

REMOVE UNUSED PROGRAMS

Any job we do, there is a right way and a wrong way. For example, to drive our car we open the garage door; start the car, foot on brake, shift selector to R and ease out of the garage. Any other course could have detrimental effects, either to the car or the garage or both. Don't ask how I know this.

Our computers also require that certain actions follow a step by step procedure. One area where computer users seem to have problems is removing unwanted or unused programs. A common misconception is that removing the icon for a program on the desktop removes the program from the computer. Take a look at the icons on the desktop, look for a small white box in the lower left corner of the icon with a black arrow in it. Any icon with the white box and arrow is called a **shortcut**. The function of the shortcut is to make it easy to open a commonly used program by clicking on the icon instead of having to click on the Start button – All Programs then searching for the program we want to use. Think of the shortcut as a street sign pointing to a particular street. If we remove the street sign, it doesn't remove the street. The shortcut is the same as that street sign. If we delete the shortcut we simply removed the sign but the program is still on our computer. One note: If the icon on the desktop does not have the white box with black arrow then it actually is a piece of the program or a file and deleting it will remove it from the computer.

Another wrong way to remove a program is to go to My Computer – C: drive – Program Files and click on a program no longer needed and delete it from the computer. What we see in Program files is only part of the program. There are sometimes hundreds of files positioned all through the computer required by that program in order to run. These files will still be in place and without the entire program and all associated files it can be almost impossible to remove the remaining parts. Trying to remove a program this way also leaves entries in the computer's registry which is a database of all programs and files on the computer. The Registry will still believe the program is there and will continue to advertise its existence on the computer.

So how do we remove a program safely? The removal of any program should start by clicking on Start – Control Panel – Add and Remove Programs in Windows XP and Start – Control Panel – Programs and

---

Grandma and Grandpa, how come you're so smart?
Shortcut: A graphical link from an icon to allow quick access to frequently used files or programs.
My computer desktop is covered with shortcuts to websites, programs, documents etc.
Right click on a website and left click on "create shortcut" to add a shortcut on the desktop to that site.
Wrong: Last time I went to the barber he gave me a shortcut by mistake.

Features in Vista and Win 7. Here a directory of all programs installed on the computer will be listed. Any legitimate program installed will contain an uninstall procedure and that is what this list displays, all the uninstall protocols for each program. Highlight a program and then click on Remove in XP or Uninstall in VISTA and Win 7. Follow the prompts to complete the removal of the program. This way all the files and the registry entries for that program will be removed.

What can we do if we didn't follow the steps above and now we can't uninstall a program and error messages keep popping up that tell us things like program x could not call xyz.dll or other nonsensical messages? One way is to reinstall the program completely and then use the Add and Remove or Uninstall feature to uninstall the complete program. Certain companies, such as Norton, HP and others apparently have failed uninstalls frequently enough that they provide what I like to call a brute force uninstaller. Check on the software maker's website to see if there is a brute force uninstaller available for the program that refuses to uninstall, download it and run it to remove stubborn programs.

Many programs in the list can be uninstalled but the recommendation is that if we don't know what the program is, before uninstalling it use one of our favorite search engines to find out what the program is and whether or not it is necessary. For example if I were to uninstall Realtek High Definition Audio driver because it doesn't sound like anything I use, I would find that I no longer had sound coming from my computer.

One last note Microsoft deploys via Windows Updates, Service Packs for Windows operating systems. For the vast majority of users this will be a transparent update with no problems. However, there are a few situations which can cause problems, the worst being that after the install, the computer will not start. I do recommend that the Update be installed, but if it comes up, carefully follow the suggestions from Microsoft on preparations before the Update is installed.

Now how do I uninstall the stain on my shirt?

SOMETIMES: BRUTE FORCE – THE ONLY ANSWER

Finesse is our first effort to complete any task we attempt. To open an olive jar, we grab the lid and give it a twist. No luck and we grab it tighter and twist harder. Still no success, so we get out the rubber lid holder and reef on it some more. Still no joy? Grab the lid pliers and watch as we tear paint off the lid but the jar stays sealed. Now try running it under hot water and twist it again. Still it resists our endeavors with a mocking lack of movement. No more mister nice guy. We grab a butter knife from the drawer and not so gently tap dents all around the edge of the lid. Call it the brute force removal. This usually does the trick. The lid spins off and the olives are ours.

Computers working well allow us to uninstall programs with adroit and artful management. Legitimate programs that we load on our computers also put an uninstall module on the hard drive so that should we decide the program doesn't meet our needs we can uninstall it without problems. Installed programs have folders, files and registry entries throughout the computer that must be removed if the decision is made to uninstall a program. The program's own uninstall module is designed to remove all these pieces thoroughly leaving the computer clean and ready for our next installation. How do we know if a program we installed also loaded an uninstall feature? Click on START – CONTROL PANEL and then Add/Remove programs (XP) or Programs and Features. (Vista/Windows 7) A list of all properly installed programs will appear. This list is actually a link to the Uninstall feature for each program listed. By clicking on the program and then Remove (XP) Uninstall (Vista/Windows 7) the module nimbly removes all the components of the program. This is the proper way and should always be the first method attempted to remove a program. Do not delete files and folders as this does not remove all the pieces of the program. Should we delete the uninstall module, then the pieces of the program can never be deleted, short of reinstalling the program to **reinstall** the uninstall needed to remove the program. (Martha, say that three times real fast.)

But alas, it is not a perfect world. Sometimes, bad things happen to good software. Occasionally a program will refuse to uninstall. Or worse some of it will uninstall and parts will remain. So what? A perfect example is when we change from one Anti-Virus brand to another. Almost without exception, the instructions for

Grandma and Grandpa, how come you're so smart?
Reinstall: Installation of a program that previously existed on a computer.
I removed a program because it might be causing problems then reinstalled it after determining it wasn't.
I accidently uninstalled a program I used so I reinstalled by running the setup program.
Wrong: I backed the car out of the garage then reinstalled it when I returned from my trip.

installation require that we remove any old anti-virus software currently running on the computer. If we don't get the old software completely uninstalled we discover that not only can we not install the new software, but often we cannot reinstall the old. One might think that this happens rarely, but every antivirus company I am familiar with provides a butter knife to tap around the edges. In tech talk it is more commonly known as a Brute Force Uninstaller or BFU. The BFU is a scripting program that executes a series of preset commands such as remove this registry entry, remove this file, remove this folder etc. Companies providing the BFU have the scripts written to remove each part of their program.

Rarely are the BFU's included with the software we download or purchase. But they are usually available at the website for the software that is posing the problems. For example, Norton Antivirus provides on their support site their version of a BFU for those instances where we cannot remove their software. If we go to a company's website and click on the support tab, we can type in the search field, uninstaller and locate the BFU we need. HP provides BFUs for removing stubborn printer software and so on. Sometimes though a company will not provide a BFU, but our friends at Microsoft provide a general BFU to get us over any rough spots. The MS BFU is called the Program Install and Uninstall troubleshooter and provides a tool that removes most of the programs but more importantly the registry entries related to each specific program. The Cleanup Utility can be downloaded for free from support.microsoft.com/mats/Program_Install_and_Uninstall. Always start with the Add/Remove or Programs and Features in Control Panel first, then look for a specific BFU and use the Program Install and Uninstall troubleshooter as a last resort.

Now where's that butter knife?

RESTORE OR RECOVER? BE CAREFUL WHAT YOU ASK FOR

"It ain't over till its over," said Yogi Berra, known for his propensity to create malapropisms with little effort. Malapropisms are the unintentional but usually funny use of the wrong but similar sounding word when expressing a thought. President Bush gave Yogi a run for his money with malapropisms such as "One of the things important about history is to remember the true history." In the computer world, there are great opportunities for malapropisms, some funny, some disastrous if we act on them. The word "Malapropism" is derived from a French phrase meaning "badly for the purpose."

There are two words in the computer universe that are often interchanged but have entirely different meanings. System Restore and **System Recovery**. Both sound beneficial but result in completely different results if we act on them.

System Restore first appeared in Windows ME in the late 1990's. This was an effort by Microsoft to allow a user to undo changes that negatively impacted the operation of the computer. For example, if we load a new program and suddenly the printer won't work or we can't hear sounds then something has altered the state of our computer and not for the better. One avenue we can take is to use System RESTORE to put the state of the computer back to its condition before we loaded the egregious software. System restore does not alter any of our data files, letters, spreadsheets, pictures or emails. So if you accidently delete that 1200 page manuscript that is the life story of the greatest person in the world, System Restore will not make it magically reappear. System Restore takes a full snapshot of the registry and some dynamic system files and creates restore points every time we alter our computer. New updates, new programs, new hardware etc generates a new restore point identified by date. It is then possible to return a computer to a previous point in time before a change occurred. Install new software, use system restore to go back to a date prior to the installation, reboot the PC and the new software is no longer there.

How to run a system restore? Open System Restore by clicking the Start button, click on All Programs, then clicking Accessories, under Accessories click System Tools, and then click System Restore. A screen will appear asking if you want to create a restore point or restore the computer to an earlier date. Choose Restore to an

> **Grandma and Grandpa, how come you're so smart?**
> **System Recovery:** The return of a computer to its original state after purchase.
> Use a system recovery to eliminate all programs, files and add an operating system prior to donating it.
> There is a huge difference between a system recovery and a system restore.
> Wrong: Ordered a pizza delivered as a system recovery for the burned meatloaf.

earlier date. Click next and a calendar will appear with dates that contain restore points in bold. Pick a date prior to the fractious installation and then follow the steps. The computer will restart, some time will be required for the computer to make all the changes and then it will start and tell us whether or not the restore process was successful. System Restore is operating by default on all computers, however there are times when System Restore is turned off which deletes all the restore points on the computer. To verify System Restore is turned on follow the steps above, if the program opens and calendar displays bold dates it is working. If System Restore is not turned on then no time traveling to a happier day will be possible. Note: System Restore does not restore personal files so do not confuse it with a backup. (Backup? Martha, he's mentioned that before.)

Now that we have a bead on System Restore, what is a System Recovery? Many years ago, computers shipped with a set of recovery disks which most folks promptly lost. Today, these same recovery disks are hidden on a secret partition on the hard drive. Many manufactures incorporate a set of key strokes required when their company logo appears at start up to boot into the Recovery Partition. Newer Vista and Windows 7 machines can boot to a screen that offers Repair Windows as a choice. From this choice will be the option to Recover the Computer. A System Recovery formats the C:\ partition (where all the programs and files are) and then reinstalls the operating system and all the software that was originally on the PC. Or put another way, all our files, pictures, music, third party programs, updates or anything else we put on the computer after we bought it are gone never to be seen again.

System Restore is time travel, System Recovery is starting new. Restore, Recovery where do you want to go today?

THE HUNT IS ON!

The hunt is on. Where is that picture or document we saved? What was it called? Don't remember where we put it and don't remember what we named it? We have hundreds if not thousands of pictures and documents saved on our computer and it will take years to look through them all. There has to be a simpler way.

Even with Windows XP there were mechanisms for finding the file that didn't want to be found. Click on Start then search. The dialogue box that appeared offered to search just for photographs, or documents or all files and folders. It offered to search specific places or the entire computer. We could narrow the search by inputting a time frame inside which we believe the file was created, last week, last month, within the last year or since the computer was first turned on.

Vista and Windows 7 refined this capability even further. Click on the Start button and a search box appears immediately above the Start button. Start typing in the Start menu search box and instantly a list of relevant files on your PC appears. We can search by typing the name of the file, or based on its tags, file type, and even contents. To see even more matches, click a category in the results, like Documents or Pictures, or click See more results. Our search terms are **highlighted** to make it easier to scan the list.

Don't remember exactly the name of the document? Know that it was created in Microsoft word. Type *.doc in the search box and a list of documents will appear. (* is a wild card that tells the computer to search for anything and in our example the .doc would indicate that any file found must have that extension.)

The content search is very useful. I have a database of hundreds of columns written over the last six years. If I need to reference a previous column about a particular subject I can type that subject term or phrase in the search box and Windows will search the entire computer for any documents containing that term or phrase in the body of the document.

Windows search is also available within each folder on the computer. For example, open the Documents folder. In the top right corner is a search box that we can utilize to search the contents of that folder. If I type

> **Grandma and Grandpa, how come you're so smart?**
> **Highlighted:** To emphasize or make prominent.
> Highlighting a word or paragraph allows us to copy or delete or move the selected area.
> When listing the results of a search, Vista and Windows 7 highlights the word that triggered that selection.
> Wrong: At the top of Mt Everest, Tom stood in the sun and considered himself highlighted.

in 'spy' any document that has the word spy or any word that contains within it the letters spy such as spyglass or spying is immediately brought up in a list.

Consider when searching that "less is more." If I type in the box 'antivirus' the computer searches for documents that contain that word or any word that has that complete string of letters within it. If I type in only anti, the list of results will contain antivirus, antimalware, anti gravity, antispyware etc. If we wish to narrow our results add more to the search requirement. Still not finding what we want? Scroll to the bottom of the results page for more search locations including the Internet.

Files can run but they cannot hide.

NEW PC? TRANSFER FILES FROM OLD TO NEW

Just a few days to go now and there under the Christmas tree is a big box with our name on it. It sure looks like the exact size of that new computer we asked Santa for. Isn't there some tradition that allows presents to be opened on the eve of Christmas Eve? The suspense is torturous. It has to be that computer with Windows 7, tons of Ram, oodles of hard drive space and lots of nifty USB ports all over it for adding really important stuff like cameras and flash drives. (Martha, it better not be a paisley tie.)

Not that we are trying to figure out what our present is, but it might be prudent to prepare a game plan for setting up a new computer. Not that we know for sure that's what's in the big box with some letters just visible under the paper, is that a DE or maybe an H and a P? Just assuming it is a computer what should we do after we rip off the wrapping paper and throw it at our siblings?

First thing to decide is whether we need to move files and settings from our old computer to the new one. Microsoft provides a very efficient program for doing just that. It is called Windows Easy Transfer. Windows Easy Transfer helps you transfer personal files, e-mail, data, files, media, and settings from your old computer to the new one. If we are transferring to a new Windows 7 pc, Windows Easy Transfer is already included on the PC.

Set up the new computer, work through the opening "Welcome to your new computer," screens until the desktop is ready for action. Plug in the Flash Drive or external hard drive and click on the Start Flag – Programs – Accessories - **System Tools**, then Windows Easy Transfer. Click on the Start Button and type in Windows Easy Transfer. The program will start and ask if this is the new or old PC. It will ask if the transfer is to be accomplished via a network connection, Transfer Cable, USB Flash Drive or external drive or DVD. It then asks if Windows Easy Transfer is installed on the old PC and if not insert a USB drive and the program will put a Windows Easy Transfer installer on the USB Drive. Move the drive to the old computer and Windows Easy Transfer will be installed on the old computer and the transfer of files will begin using the method previously specified.

> **Grandma and Grandpa, how come you're so smart?**
> **System Tools:** Collection of software for information, maintenance and performing system tasks.
> System Tools contains Disk Cleanup used to remove temporary files and other unneeded files.
> To identify a program using excessive memory use Resource Monitor found in System Tools.
> Wrong: Each morning before work I consider shaving cream, soap and toilet paper as system tools.

For those with only one computer in the house it is very easy to use a Flash Drive or even an external hard drive if you have one available. Windows Easy Transfer then surveys the old computer and tells us how big the transfer file will be. For most folks it is fairly small and doesn't pose any problems, but if it is more than sixteen gigs it will require either the external hard drive or a network connection to the new computer to complete the task.

Windows Easy Transfer can take some time to complete the gathering of our files and settings so be patient. There is a progress bar that can at times, seem to be moving at the pace of a snail in molasses but it will finish eventually. Once it is done, disconnect the transfer device, power down the old computer and move it out of the way. On the new PC Windows Easy Transfer creates a report that lists everything that was copied from the old to the new computer.

It will copy our screen saver, our background, pictures documents, email settings etc. Note however, it will not copy programs. So there is a great game on the old computer that occupies hours of time, it will not be on the new computer unless we have the disk to reinstall it with.

Finally, the printer needs to be installed. Make a note to NOT hook up the printer to the computer until the install disk tells us to. Connecting the printer with out the software in place can lead to all kinds of problems and may result in having to call in a tech to make it work.

Have a Merry Christmas, and if it turns out to be a paisley tie, smile and say thank you anyway.

CUT, COPY AND PASTE

Almost two decades have passed since computers started to make their way into our homes and businesses. Typewriters disappeared, mimeographs were melted down and printers became ubiquitous. In all that time it seems that one of the easiest functions to perform has been hidden from many PC users. We speak of the ability to move text, pictures or files from one place to another.

Often when explaining how to take a picture and move it into a document I will say, "Just copy and paste it here." The user will look bewildered and profess to never having learned how to copy and paste. For them it is magic. But it has been around for decades. Think of the days when newspapers were all laid up by hand. A person would carefully copy the reporter's hand written stories into metal type that would then "copy" the words to a piece of paper that became the newspaper. Today we can do this electronically in moments instead of hours. Let's try to **copy and paste** some text.

Take your mouse, and place your cursor at the beginning of the text we wish to copy, then click and hold the left mouse button, while pulling your mouse over the text. This will highlight the text. Now release the left mouse button. Notice the text remained highlighted. With the cursor over the highlighted text, right click the mouse for a context menu that will give us a group of options. Select 'copy'. Now place the cursor where you want to put the copied text. It can be in the same document, an e-mail, a different document even a different program. Right click your mouse again, and select 'paste' and you will have copied and pasted the text.

Don't forget to use some shortcuts to save time. In any document or webpage, if we double click on a word the word will be highlighted and we can continue with our copy and paste procedure. Triple click on a word and the entire paragraph it is contained in will be highlighted. There are some more shortcuts below.

Cut and paste is the same as above, except you choose 'cut', instead of 'copy'.

Shortcuts
To Highlight: Press 'Ctrl' + 'A'.

Grandma and Grandpa, how come you're so smart?
Copy and Paste: Copy a section of one document and then place it (paste) in another document.
Preparing the newsletter, I copy and pasted the minutes from the secretary's e-mail to the newsletter.
Copy by highlighting a word, paragraph entire page then paste it to another document or e-mail.
Wrong: My friend made a snowball and threw it in my face and I copied and pasted him back.

To Copy: Highlight an area, as shown above, then hold 'Ctrl' + 'C' (For Mac users 'Apple' + 'C').
To Paste: Click your mouse where you want the text pasted, and then press 'Ctrl' + 'V'
(For Mac users 'Apple' + 'S'.)

The ability to cut, copy, and paste is found in most programs. Sometimes, the ability to do these tasks via the mouse is disabled, but is still quickly achieved through the use of the shortcuts outlined above.

If using context menus to accomplish this task proves cumbersome or difficult, we can after we have highlighted the text we want to copy and paste, click on the Edit menu and from there select copy and then move to the destination for the copied text, click the Edit menu again and select paste.

These same steps can be used for copying or moving files from one location to another. For practice open up My Pictures (XP) or Pictures. (Vista and Windows 7) Click on the picture or pictures we want to move to another folder or place in a document. Right mouse click on the highlighted pictures and select copy from the context menu. Now navigate to the folder or document we want the pictures to be in and right mouse click again and select Paste.

Remember, Copy makes a duplicate of the text or file, while Cut removes the text or file from the original position and pastes it in the new location.

LEAVE NO TRACKS FOR SAFETY'S SAKE

Another year. What awaits is anybody's guess. Our computers are cleaned up, backed up and raring to go. Social networks like Facebook and LinkedIn are making everyone friends with everyone else. Folks post information they wouldn't tell their mothers, to the web for all to see. **YouTube** has created the largest library of video clips in history. Want to know how to do something? Surf over to youtube.com, and in the search field type in "changing the fan belt on a VW without turning off the engine." There is a video demonstrating how to do it. Want to breed crickets, yup that's there too.

Fact is there exist almost everything and anything imaginable available for viewing or downloading. But sometimes things we want to see may not be something others should know we examined. For example: Traveling we may look up on a public computer our bank accounts or the telephone numbers of friends and family. We wouldn't want the next person to use the computer to have access to any of that information. Perhaps we visit a sick loved one and surreptitiously use their computer to look up a symptom or medicine and wouldn't want them to be upset thinking about our query. Let's be honest, even at work a few have used the company's computer to check airline ticket prices or post a resume online. Companies frown on use of equipment for personal reasons. Folks have even been fired for improper use of a computer because they left tracks and histories of everyplace they were on the Internet.

Remember when Caller ID came out on telephones so everyone would know who was on the phone? It was immediately followed by Caller ID Blocking, just dial 67 before the call and your id doesn't appear, so no one knows whose calling. Internet browsers; Internet Explorer, Firefox, Chrome and Safari just to mention the most commonly used browsers all track where we go for convenience. They make it easy for us to return to sites we have visited, record how many times we visited and even create a favorite or bookmark to make it speedy to go back to a particular site. Even the questions we type into search fields are recorded and used for making the Internet more relevant to more users.

> **Grandma and Grandpa, how come you're so smart?**
> **YouTube:** Video sharing Web site that lets anyone upload short videos for private or public viewing.
> Many organizations post short videos to YouTube to promote their events.
> A video such as those on YouTube that are viewed by millions of people are said to have gone viral.
> Wrong: Do YouTube that river often?

Thankfully all the companies that provide these browsers recognize a need for privacy. Not everything we do is for public consumption. As such they all have a mechanism for turning off all the recording a browser normally does and allows the user to surf the web anonymously. Internet Explorer calls it InPrivate Browsing, Firefox and Safari labels it Private Browsing Mode, Chrome describes it as the Incognito window. They all serve the same purpose. Choosing this mode to surf the web enables us to surf the web without leaving a trail in the browser. This helps prevent anyone else who might be using our computer from seeing where we visited and what we looked at on the web.

To enable InPrivate for Internet Explorer, open a new tab and click on InPrivate Browsing or click on Safety and then InPrivate Browsing. For Chrome, click on the file menu and select New Incognito Window. To enable Private Browsing in Firefox, click on Tools (in the menu bar) and then select Start Private Browsing. A popup menu appears asking if you would really like to start Private Browsing mode. Hit the "Start Private Browsing" button to continue.

Each of the browsers display a caption near the address of each site visited reminding us that we are in a private mode. This is because while in this mode, the browser will continue to collect some cookies and other information required to display the pages we visit, but at the end of the session, when we close the window all traces of our visit will be deleted. This means cookies, temporary Internet files, webpage history, passwords, address bar, search and AutoComplete data, will be deleted after we close the browser window. (Martha, you can start shopping at work again.)

This is a great tool to add to your bag of tricks, especially when traveling. It allows us to move stealthily over the WEB, to be discreet, to pussyfoot around. Should you forget to trigger InPrivate Browsing when traveling and using public computers, make sure to click on the Safety button and then Delete Browsing History to accomplish almost the same thing.

Who goes there?

CLOUD COMPUTING

Can we extend the usefulness of an older PC? We've considered a shiny new computer but our faithful digital servant still fires up, still connects to the Internet and retrieves our email, alas it seems just at a slower pace. We still have that Windows XP machine purchased seven years ago and we hate to replace it just because it seem a bit slow. Is there a way to stretch out its life and boost its performance a little bit?

Perusing some past columns, I came across one written about five years ago on this very topic. In it were a plethora of free programs from anti virus to office suites that would give the same functionality as new machines of the time. They could be downloaded from the Internet and installed on our PCs. But times they are a changing. What worked then may not be the best approach today. If an older PC is sitting on the desk, click on the START button, then use a right mouse click on My Computer. A menu will appear and left click on Properties. A new window appears and down towards the bottom right it will tell us the amount of RAM memory we have. Yours may have 256 megs of RAM, later years may have 512 or perhaps even one gig of memory.

What is RAM (**Random Access Memory**)? Think of it this way. Go to the kitchen and look at the cabinets. The drawers and cupboards are like the hard drive in a PC. They store things. Now consider we are the RAM memory. Nothing in the drawers can do anything unless we open the drawer and take something out to bake that favorite cake. How fast we get that cake done depends on how fast we can retrieve and use the instruments of construction. But what if we also had to make a soup and a salad? Set the table, pour drinks, dice potatoes, add seasoning, prepare sandwiches for work etc. It would take longer to complete all these items. RAM memory in a computer is the same. The more it has to do the longer it takes to complete a task.

Computer manufactures have increased the amount of RAM memory that comes with a new machine. In our analogy, it would be akin to adding another cook in the kitchen. Twice as many cooks, half the time to complete all the tasks. But in the case of our computers, the folks that create those wonderful programs we like to use know there are more cooks in the kitchen so they add more dishes to the menu. The programs do much

> **Grandma and Grandpa, how come you're so smart?**
> **Random Access Memory: (RAM)** A type of computer memory that can be accessed randomly.
> Programs and processes run in RAM while files and pictures are stored on the hard drive.
> Both the hard drive and RAM are referred to as memory but one should be memory and one storage.
> Wrong: Opening and closing drawers and cabinets, I was using my random access memory to find my pen.

more than they used to, but require much more RAM to do it. Compare our 256 or 512 meg machines of yesteryear with a new Windows 7 PC today. At minimum, these new machines come with two gigs of memory or eight times the memory of a 2001 PC. Many new machines are coming with four, six and even eight gigs of RAM memory. Software programmers are writing programs to use it all. If we load programs written for two or more gigs on a PC with only 512 megs of RAM, we understand why it slows down.

What can we do if we want to hang on to the older PC for a while longer? One approach would be to take advantage of CLOUD computing. CLOUD computing utilizes programs that reside and run on some super computer on the Internet. We use the programs as if they were resident but all we are doing is viewing the results of the program as it completes each task assigned to it. This requires a connection to the Internet which almost everyone has today. We could remove everything from our computer except the operating system, a web browser and a few browser add-ons like Java, Shockwave, Flash and do virtually all our tasks in the CLOUD. Here is an example: Surf over to docs.google.com. If we don't have a Google account it takes less than five minutes to create one and it is FREE. (Martha, that word sends tingles to my toes.) We can write a letter, start a spreadsheet, create a presentation and more as if it was running on our PC. Virtually an entire office suite of programs and not one uses RAM on our PC. Microsoft offers a similar feature called Office Web Apps that is part of Skydrive. Sign up for a Live account from Microsoft and start using the Web Apps.

Do you read your email in a web browser? That is using the CLOUD for email. Want to edit some pictures? www.photoshop.com is a free online photo editing site from Adobe that not only allows cropping, red eye removal and many other features but will store up to two gigs worth of pictures online all for no charge.

Online Storage is another feature for the cloud. There are many companies that offer to backup and store files and data to the Cloud. Mozyhome, Carbonite, Norton Online Backup, Dell Online Backup are just a few available. Microsoft also has Skydrive that allows us to store twenty five gigs of data for free. There is also Windows Live Mesh that can automatically sync files from our computer to Skydrive or to another computer anywhere in the world. Dropbox (www.dropbox.com) will install a small program on the computer that will then automatically store files online. A nice touch with dropbox is that it creates a virtual drive on the computer that we can drag and drop files into as if they were just moving around our computer but in fact are being stored online. Dropbox provides two gigs of storage for free and larger size storage capability at reasonable prices.

Pictures can also be stored in the Cloud at places like www.picasa.com, www.snapfish.com, or www.shutterfly.com just to name a few. From there they can be reviewed, emailed, put into albums or sent to a printer.

Another advantage to CLOUD computing is that if we create and store items on the web, when the day comes that our old calculating companion keels over with little sparks fading away, our new digital domestique will connect to the Internet and find everything we have done just as we left it.

Mother told me my head was in the clouds.

STATUS BAR IS GOOD FOR BAG OF BROWSER TRICKS

A conversation this week started with, "do you use the status bar in your browser?" Answer: What is a browser? Let's define browser. A web browser is a software application for retrieving, presenting, and traversing information resources on the World Wide Web. Or for most of us, a browser is opened when we click on Internet Explorer or Mozilla Firefox or Google Chrome. This is the program we use to surf the web, buy airline tickets, shop online, check our webmail and many other functions.

There are some features built into these browsers that are very useful. One of the functions that we should note and use is called the status bar. Since most folks use Internet Explorer we will use that as our example but other browsers have very similar features.

Grab a cup of coffee and open up Internet Explorer. Look at the bottom of the window. Is there a bar running along the bottom of the window? If not, then use the right mouse to click on the top of the window. A menu of choices will appear. Look for **Status Bar**. If there is no check mark next to it, use the left mouse button to click on it to activate the Status Bar at the bottom of the window. What does the Status Bar tell us?

Far to the right are a percentage and a magnifying glass. This is a zoom control. If there is something on the screen that is just a bit too small to see clearly we can click on the magnifying glass and zoom in up to 400 %. If we don't return the zoom to normal and close the browser window it will remember the zoom status the next time we open the browser.

The left side of the Status Bar communicates several things of importance. Watch the left side of the Status Bar. As we search the web each time we go to another site, the Status Bar may tell us that the Page is Loading

> **Grandma and Grandpa, how come you're so smart?**
> **Status Bar:** Bar at the bottom of a browser window displaying variety of information about the website.
> Before clicking a hyperlink on a website hold the mouse over it, and look at the status bar for the real link.
> The status bar will display the progress of the browser as it loads a new website.
> Wrong: All my rich friends hang out at Pierre's, a real status bar.

or Waiting for Response from the website we are trying to go to. But more important from a safety standpoint, if we move the curser with our mouse over a hyperlink on the page, the Status Bar will show us where the link actually goes to. For example, I recently received an e-mail that purportedly was from Chase Bank thanking me for my recent transaction and if I wanted to see the details of the transaction to click on the link in the e-mail. Since I don't have a Chase account I new the e-mail was a phishing attempt, but by hovering the mouse over the link in the e-mail (do not click on the link) the Status Bar told me that the link was to a site in Romania, not www.chase.com.

Microsoft has also built the Status Bar into Windows Live Mail and it displays the actual location of a hyperlink in the same fashion for those of us that use a mail client instead of Webmail.

To be forewarned is to be forearmed. What's your Status?

TALK TO YOUR COMPUTER, MAKE IT UNDERSTAND

To enable **speech recognition** in Windows 7, open the control panel and click on Speech Recognition. A menu of options appears. The first item will start speech recognition. However, I recommend that "Set up microphone" be selected first. Use a high quality microphone. An inexpensive microphone will result in the speech recognition software misinterpreting your voice.

The next item on the list is Take Speech Tutorial. This begins training of both the computer and the user. The computer begins to interpret the inflection and accent of the user while the user begins to understand the speed and tone that they need to use for the most effective use of the Speech Recognition program. The user also learns the commands to invoke for corrections, spelling and punctuation. While possible, at the completion of the tutorial, to immediately start using the Speech Recognition tools, it is strongly recommended that the, Train Your Computer To Better Understand You, portion of the menu be exercised. The software is designed to learn from its experience with the user and the more time spent training means a more accurate interpretation of the user's speech.

Next click on Advanced Speech Options and decide if Speech Recognition should start every time the computer starts up or if it should be voice activated or manually started when we need it. What are some of the tasks we can perform with Speech Recognition besides dictating letters? We can dictate emails, open programs, shut the computer off, almost anything we can do with a mouse we can do by voice. For example: I can say, "Click Documents," and the computer will open the folder where my documents are stored. If I then say, "number," all the documents listed will be assigned a number. Next I can say, "22," and the document numbered 22 will be highlighted. If I then speak "OK" the document selected will open and I can begin to dictate changes or additions to the document.

The key component to Speech Recognition is patience and training. The more time spent with the computer training the speech recognition software the more accurate it will become. Even so the software will make mistakes. After dictating an email or letter, remember to proof read it. And remember if you pronounce "and" as "an" the computer will not know the difference and your letter may look like it was written by a third grader.

Grandma and Grandpa, how come you're so smart?
Speech Recognition: A computer program that recognizes and reacts to human speech.
Folks that have trouble working a keyboard often find they can talk to the computer and create emails.
Speech recognition should not be confused with command and response like the phones press 1 for Joe.
Wrong: When talking to tech support in India, I have a real problem with speech recognition.

Training, double checking, and final proof of documents is critical.

Busy columnists can also use voice recognition to write their columns. This column was dictated while the reading the latest computer journals and enjoying breakfast. I will review and proof the column when finished but to demonstrate the limitations of speech to text I plan to leave some of the errors in.

Voice recognition is not the same as listening to someone. For example; we can be in a crowded room with many people speaking and yet identify and focus on the conversation we are interested in. The computer's accuracy depends on our spending time reading the preparation tutorials which allow our computers to match our speech characteristics with the training data. It also means that we practice clear and concise pronunciation and that we work in a clean noise environment (e.g. quiet room or office space). This explains why some users, especially those whose speech is heavily accented, might achieve recognition rates much lower than expected.

There are several ways to acquire speech recognition for your computer. If you are a Vista or Windows XP user this capability is already built in and is installed by default with the operating system. There are third party programs such as Dragon Naturally Speaking that also allow this function. Voice recognition can be used to command your computer to perform specific actions in addition to dictation. Voice recognition can be used to create e-mail, open and close programs. Right click on the toolbar at bottom of your desktop and click on language bar to make speech recognition easily accessible. Microsoft Office activates voice recognition by clicking on tools and from the drop down menu click on Speech. This will begin the voice recognition engine and everything said after that will be printed on the page as you speak. Voice recognition becomes more accurate with use, identifying speech characteristics and allowing the user to speak at nearly a normal pace. It just requires the user to be a bit more careful pronouncing their words. (Martha, are you listening?)

I still need to go back over my document and edit for spelling and syntax errors. With speech recognition you must also look for correct word usage. The speech recognition software is not perfect as you can tell from the server which I am not a period. Notice the words in the previous sentence should read "from the paragraph which I have not edited." I can probably improve accuracy if I used a headset microphone instead of a boom MIC. This would cut down ambient noise which the microphone picks up and the computer attempts to interpret as words.

Verbally opening and closing a program is not quite as difficult for the computer because these are commands rather than random words. The computer expects commands, but has to try to interpret random words. Give it a try but be patient, it's the computer's first day at school.

Now, what was I saying?

THESE ARE A FEW OF OUR FAVORITE THINGS

These are a few of our favorite things. We have our favorite shoes, favorite jacket and even our favorite websites. Shoes are racked in closets, jackets on hangers, but our favorite websites are in one long list in our browsers. Some have hundreds of Favorites. It seems it would be faster to hunt for the website than to go to the list of Favorites and try to find the one we want. There must some way to organize these lists to facilitate locating the one website we want to visit.

Regardless of the browser we use the techniques for organizing our Favorites are the same. Internet Explorer calls them Favorites, FireFox and Chrome refer to them as Bookmarks, but the how to organize is the same. Let's look at some tips that can bring order and sanity to our lists of Favorites.

One of the simplest and easiest ways to find the Favorite we are searching for would be if they were in alphabetical order. To accomplish this, open the list of Favorites and pick any site on the list. Use the right mouse button to click on that site. This brings up a context menu of choices. From the menu use the left mouse button to click on Sort by Name and almost magically all the Favorites are now in alphabetical order.

There is more to organizing our Favorites than just putting them in order. Click on the Favorites button (Internet Explorer) or the Bookmarks button (FireFox) and then click on Organize Favorites or Bookmarks. A new window opens up and we see a list of our Favorites and some control buttons at the bottom. If we are cleaning out old **links**, click once on the first one we want to eliminate, then hold down the CTRL key and continue clicking on all the rest of the doomed links. After selecting the ones to go, click on the Delete button and they are history.

Click on the button labeled New Folder. Type in a name for the folder and press the Enter key on the keyboard. Now select all the Favorites that are common to the folder we just made. Click on the button labeled Move and then select our new folder from the list and all the websites we selected go into the folder. For example: I created a folder labeled Weather. Now I select Favorites such as NOAA, WeatherUnderground,

---

Grandma and Grandpa, how come you're so smart?
Links: Any address that when clicked on connects to another location.
Hyperlinks, favorites, bookmarks, and shortcuts are all forms of computer links.
While reading a website article about chocolate there was a link to a website devoted to chocolate recipes.
Wrong: I was so mad I took my computer to the links and beat it with a golf club, a nine iron to be exact.

NCAR and any other weather related sites, click on Move and then select the folder named Weather and all the weather related sites are in one handy folder and easy to find. We can even move a folder into another folder if we need to have subfolders. Example; our main folder may be Cars and inside that folder we create subfolders such as Ford, Chevy and so on.

Too busy to even open the browser to reach our Favorites? Put the Favorites button on the Start Menu. Right mouse click on the Start button in the lower left corner of the screen. From the menu select Properties. Click on the tab labeled Start Menu, then click on Customize. Now scroll down to the check box beside Favorites Menu and put a check mark in the box. That will put Favorites on our Start menu. In the future we can click on start, then Favorites, then the website we want to go to. A browser will open with the page desired displayed.

Organizing Favorites is one of my favorite things.

DEFINING ANTIVIRUS SOFTWARE PROTECTION

Pavlov's dog was eventually trained to salivate at the sound of a bell by repeatedly ringing a bell and then presenting the dog with food. After a while the dog would salivate at the sound of the bell even when no food was prevented. PC users are trained to install antivirus software by being told computer viruses will attack their computers, wipe hard drives, steal financial information and other wise make digital life unbearable.

What part of an antivirus program will actually protect us from evil viruses and spyware? Is it the program? If it is, then those folks that buy a computer with a thirty day trial of some antivirus and never purchase the subscription after the trial runs out are shielded from harm. Unfortunately that is not the case.

Think of an antivirus program as if it were a car. A car will carry passengers as long as there is fuel in the tank. Without fuel, the car is mechanically fine; it just won't do what it is supposed to do. The fuel of an antivirus program is called a virus definition or **virus signature**. A virus definition is a piece of binary code unique to a virus or spyware. "Virus definitions," refer to a database containing all the known computer viruses and spyware that is used by our antivirus program to detect, quarantine and remove unwanted software.

When the antivirus program on our computer does a scan it compares all our computer's content including files, hard drives, boot sectors, RAM memory and removable drives against its' virus definition database. If the program finds any code in these areas that match those in the definition database it takes appropriate action to protect our calculating companion. As new viruses or spyware (collectively referred to as malware) appear, our antivirus program receives new virus definitions that are added to the database which allows the detection of the ever expanding world of malware.

Those new definitions are what make our antivirus programs effective. If we do not renew our antivirus program subscription, as in the case of those folks that are still running the trial version that came on the computer five years ago, we do not receive virus definition updates to the database and the program does not know how to recognize new variants of malware that appear. How many new malware programs are released

Grandma and Grandpa, how come you're so smart?
Virus Signature: An algorithm or hash that uniquely identifies a specific virus.
An antivirus program useless if it doesn't receive regular virus signature updates for new viruses.
The subscription for anti virus programs is not for the program but for the updates to the virus signatures.
Wrong: He scribbled his name on the form so badly it looked like a virus signature.

each year? Why is it important to make sure we have a functioning antivirus program and have it updated automatically?

"G Data has noted a general increase in malware this year: the number of new computer viruses has already reached a new record for the first half of 2010, with 1,017,208 malware programs. Experts at G Data SecurityLabs are predicting a record total of over two million new malware programs for 2010 as a whole."

These numbers are not as frightening as they seem as many of these viruses are written poorly or mutations and rarely succeed in their mission. However it only takes one to mess up an otherwise great day. With many antivirus programs to choose from and many of them offering free versions, there is no reason not to install a current and effective program on the computer. To see a list of Microsoft recommended security programs surf over to www.microsoft.com/windows/antivirus-partners/windows-7.aspx.

Let's stay protected out there.

LOST AND FOUND OUR INTERNET CONNECTION

One of the most common calls received by computer techs is the plaintive cry, "I can't get on the Internet." Since a service call means out of pocket expense, let's examine some of the common causes for loss of an Internet connection and some simple steps to try before picking up the phone.

Most folks open their favorite web browser such as Internet Explorer, Firefox, Chrome or Safari and get the frightening message, "Page cannot be displayed." Don't panic, the web browser is only the program that allows us to visually interpret the data from the Internet. It is NOT the connection to the Internet. Think of our televisions. There are television signals constantly coming from the air, dish or cable but we cannot see our favorite shows unless we have a TV at the end of the incoming signals. Then one day we turn on the TV and get snow or no signal. It doesn't necessarily mean that our television has quit working. It might be as simple as a loose cable. The question is to find where the problem resides.

A quick way to determine if the problem is with our PC or further up the line is to **PING** a website. Click on the Start button, and then click on Run. In the text field type CMD and click OK. A black DOS window will appear with a flashing cursor. Type the following command: Ping www.yahoo.com. If the window responds with four lines that read "Reply from …" then the computer is connected to the Internet and the problem lies either with the browser or possibly the firewall. If the reply reads Destination unreachable or no reply at all, then the problem is either with the computer's network card, router, modem or our Internet provider.

For those that are using broadband connections to the Internet take a look at the Modem. This is the box that has either a TV cable attached from the wall to the modem or if using DSL a phone cord that runs from the wall plate to the modem. Make sure that all the LED lights are on. Some may be blinking but they must be on. If using DSL there is an LED usually labeled DSL. If the DSL light is not on there is no connection to the Internet. If none of the lights are on, check the power cord. Cats, dogs, and cleaning folks can accidently pull power plugs. No power, no Internet.

> **Grandma and Grandpa, how come you're so smart?**
> **PING:** The time it takes for a network packet to leave your computer, go to another one, and return.
> The PC tech opened a command window and typed ping www.yahoo.com to test network connectivity.
> It is also possible to ping a server by its IP address such as ping 67.21.208.142.
> Wrong: The high note she sang preceded the ping of the glass breaking.

Many people have more than one computer in the house and utilize a Router to split the Internet signal for use by multiple computers. If the modem is working, check the router to be sure that all the LED lights are lit up. If not, check power. If they are, pull the plug on the router, count to 5 and plug it back in. Wait about 15 seconds and try to reach the Internet again.

If we are still convinced that one of the hardware pieces to this puzzle is at fault but not sure which one then try restarting (rebooting) the modem, router and computer. Remember to reboot the devices according to MR. C. This is an acronym to help us remember the order in which to restart our devices. Turn off the computer, unplug the router and unplug the modem. (those with the triple play modem will need to press the reset button on the back of the modem because it has a battery backup built in and unplugging the modem will not restart it until the battery wears down) Now restart each device according to MR. C. Start by turning on the modem. Wait until the lights are flashing or solid. Next up is the router, again waiting for all the lights to come on. Now fire up the computer and test the Internet connection with a ping or opening up a browser window.

Finally, one more thing that rears its ugly head too many times to be coincidence, check that the browser has not been flagged to work offline. Open Internet Explorer for example and click on File. There is an option to work offline. This might be useful for company presentations or building websites, but for users that don't know it is there it can cost them a service call. No one has ever explained how it gets checked, but it does.

Try these solutions first, call a tech last.

GUARDING AGAINST E-MAIL SCAMS

Regular reader Tom writes,"… do a piece on an E-Mail scam that I've now seen 3 times. It involves an "acquaintance or friend" who sends a note that they've been stranded in England or Spain without any money to cover their expenses and ask for a couple of thousand dollars to help them out of their situation. My first reaction when reading these E-Mails is that they are a scam. My main concern is that this must happen when someone's E-Mail account is hacked and realize that I do not know how to avoid this or what should be done if it happens. A friend who was the latest victim had the same reaction and was having a difficult time correcting the situation. Are there any precautionary steps that should be taken (e.g. is Web Mail more susceptible than client based) and where would someone start to correct the problem?)"

Tom is correct, these e-mails are scams. Also correct is that the sender's e-mail account has been hacked. This simply means a nefarious character has managed to access the e-mail account by guessing the password and sends a bogus money request to everyone in the account's e-mail address book. As the recipient of these spurious e-mails it frustrates us that we cannot prevent them from showing up in our inbox.

What steps should we take if these sham e-mails appear in our inbox? First: contact the owner of the e-mail address that sent the note and inform them their e-mail account has been compromised, preferably by phone because the hacked e-mail account may no longer be accessible to the rightful owner. Suggest that if possible they should immediately change their e-mail password. Changing the password will usually stop the phony e-mails.

It makes no difference whether the e-mail is being received via **webmail** or a client based e-mail program such as Windows Live Mail, Outlook or Thunderbird because the problem exist on the sender's side not the recipient's side. Should the rightful account owner be unable to establish control over their e-mail account, then as the recipient the only option would be to mark that e-mail address as spam and have our e-mail provider block it automatically.

Microsoft's e-mail products now have a feature available that allows us to mark an e-mail with "My Friend's Been Hacked." As Microsoft explains, "Our compromise detection system is always working in the background

---

Grandma and Grandpa, how come you're so smart?
Webmail: Webmail is an email service that allows you to access and send email from a Web browser.
One great advantage to webmail is the ability to access our mail from any PC connected to the Internet.
Webmail requires no PC side mail client such as Outlook or Thunderbird.
Wrong: The lady spider went looking for her future webmail.

to detect unusual behavior. When we detect bad behavior from an account (like an account that suddenly starts sending spam), we mark that account as compromised. It's a bit like your credit card company putting a hold on your account when they detect suspicious activity.

When you report that your friend's account has been compromised, Hotmail takes that report and combines it with the other information from the compromise detection engine to determine if the account in question has in fact been hijacked. It turns out that the report that comes from you can be one of the strongest "signals" to the detection engine, since you may be the first to notice the compromise. So, when you help out this way, it makes a big difference! Once we mark the account as compromised, two things happen:

•First and foremost, the account can no longer be used by the spammer.

•When your friend attempts to access their account, they're put through an account recovery flow that helps them take back control of the account.

Initially, this feature only let you report Hotmail accounts that were compromised. But it worked really well – we got thousands of reports of compromised accounts. Of course, we didn't want to stop there; we wanted to go a step farther and make it work for any email account. After all, even if you're a Hotmail user, you probably get email from friends using other email providers, and those accounts can get compromised, too.

We did the work to enable other email providers like Yahoo! and Gmail to receive these compromise reports from Hotmail including those submitted by you, and those providers will now be able to use the reports in their own systems to recover hacked accounts.

So now, in Hotmail, you can report any email account as compromised, and Hotmail will provide the compromise information to both Yahoo! and Gmail."

Prior planning can prevent our e-mail account from being hacked or if it is broken into some preliminary steps can ensure that we regain ownership. First and foremost, a strong password is critical. Letters, capitalized and lowercase, numbers and symbols should be part of any password. Next, every e-mail provider requires secret questions and answers and we should know the questions and the correct answer. Write it down and tape it to the side or back of the monitor if necessary. Finally, many providers are now asking for a phone number be added to the account information. This is used to prove ownership of an account. The provider will call that number and issue a pin number we enter to regain control of the account. What makes these items important is that many e-mail providers no longer offer phone support for their e-mail users.

Control what belongs to us or someone else will.

CHECK THE HYPERLINK TO PREVENT BEING PHISHED

The word of the day is Hyperlink. What is a hyperlink? It is a word, symbol, picture or other item that links a document to another place in the same document or to a totally different document, even one located miles or continents away. An analogy might be the light switch on the wall. If you move the switch one way it links to a light bulb somewhere and the light goes on. When surfing the Internet, we might see a link to a news feature we want to read. By clicking on the hyperlink or link as it is referred too, we are taken to the place where that article is stored. The link can be an address like www.bitsandbytesonline.com or it can be a button that says Submit or even a picture of our favorite celebrity which starts a video of their latest outrageous stunt.

Another place we see hyperlinks is in our emails. Receive an email from one of the large department stores with a "Click here to view this week's specials," and we jump from our email to the store's website. That is a hyperlink. Why is this important? Take a look at the following email I received from someone that I went to high school with.

"How are you doing, I am sorry I didn't inform you about my travelling to Africa for a seminar called Empowering Youth to Fight Racism and Bringing HIV /AIDS Education to Health. I need your help urgent because i forgot my little bag where my money and my ticket were kept. i need your help because i am having a problem with the hotel bills. I am now owning a hotel bill of $1700. I also need an extra $1000 to feed and to help myself back home. If you can help me with an amount of $2,700 and i will definitely pay you back when i return."

Fortunately I know this person and thought this was an odd email, so I called them and sure enough they had been getting calls all day from everyone in their email address book about the trip to Africa. Someone had stolen their Yahoo email account and once they had that, they used it to solicit funds from everybody in the address book. How did they get the account information? She had received an email from "Yahoo" telling her that her account had been suspended for unusual activity and to click on the **HYPERLINK** to go to Yahoo security and log in and change her password. She did exactly as asked. However the email wasn't from Yahoo

Grandma and Grandpa, how come you're so smart?
Hyperlink: A graphic or a piece of text in an Internet document that can connect readers to another webpage, or another portion of a document.
Hyperlinks are usually a bright color blue and underlined.
Reading about World War II, I follow hyperlinks to maps, aerial photos, treaties and personal diaries.
Wrong: When the cat saw the ball of yarn it became a hyperlinks and chased it around the room.

even though it had the Yahoo logo, appearance and official wording. And the link took her to another fake Yahoo page where she dutifully entered her user id and Yahoo password. The criminals then used her information to change the password on the account so she couldn't even get in to try to regain control over the account. This is known as a Phishing attack. What does this have to do with Hyperlinks?

Here are some tips to prevent this from happening to you. First and foremost, no legitimate company will ask for personal information such as logins and passwords. They may send you an email such as the one I received from PayPal reminding me that my credit card on file with them had expired. They also explained that I had to open a browser window and go to www.paypal.com to log in and make any changes. No link to PayPal provided. Another interesting trick is to hold the mouse over a link in an email and look at the bottom of the window. There will be a line there that tells us where that link really goes. If my friend had looked at that information in the fake Yahoo email, she would have seen that the hyperlink actually pointed at a site in Nigeria.

Internet Explorer 7 and higher, Firefox and most other newer Internet browsers all have phishing filters built in, and many Antivirus Suites also have phishing filters. For example, IE 7 will turn the address bar red if it detects links in a webpage that do not go where they appear to go. Don't bet the farm that they will catch everything, just use some common sense.

Be careful out there.

RUMOR CONTROL OR HOW TO LOOK LIKE AN IDIOT

I love rumors. This political silly season has seen some absolutely marvelous stories passed off as fact. Our computers allow information to be disseminated at the speed of light without regard to its veracity. Photo shop allows pictures to be modified to the point where the old adage, a picture never lies, just isn't true anymore. For example, right after the shuttle Columbia burned up on re-entry, photos supposedly taken by an Israeli satellite showed the explosion of the shuttle in orbit. Interestingly, the photos looked exactly like the opening scene from the 1998 movie Armageddon.

Documents purporting to support stories can be dummied up and posted on the Internet for those that actually take a cursory interest in finding truth. Worse still are the email forwarders. Without so much as a transitory question, they hit the forward button and send on the latest claptrap as if our world depended on this critical information. There are, as our poker friends would say, tells in these emails that give away their insincerity. Phrases like "please forward this email to everyone," or "send this to ten people," or "AOL will send you $250 for every person you send the email to."

Is there in truth no beauty? Some of these rumors, stories, pictures are crafted with just enough truth, mixed with a little current technical mumbo jumbo, throw in some emotional heartstring pulling, a number of suspected biases and we fall for it hook, line and sinker. We love the ones that say, I got this from my brother and he is a lawyer… These tomes have even gained the moniker of **Urban Legends**. Listening to a radio talk show recently, a woman called in and told the show host a fantastic story about one of the presidential candidates. Even the host of the show was shocked by the information. He asked the woman the source of the revelation. When she answered that she had read it on the Internet so it must be true he hung up.

Perhaps we need to just hang up. I know of two people who apparently questioned my political leanings and felt sure that a few truths emailed would set me straight. I confirmed the authenticity and then emailed back that I would accept verified information, but blatant lies were not appreciated. Haven't heard from them since. Not sure what that means but I like it. (Martha, can I email your cousin?)

> **Grandma and Grandpa, how come you're so smart?**
> **Urban Legends:** Modern folklore consisting of stories usually believed by their tellers to be true.
> In a famous urban legend, Microsoft and AOL will pay $250 per e-mail we send. If True why work?
> Enormous effort is made to debunk urban legends while even less effort is expended believing them.
> Wrong: Bollixed by the truth the story teller climbed a skyscraper and jumped off that urban legend fell.

So how do we know what is and isn't? Once again our computers can be rumor control. There are quite a few sites dedicated to tracking down a rumor and proving it true or false. Probably the most well known myth tester is www.snopes.com. Here we can type in the main fact of the story and find out not only if it is true or false, but when it started, and what was used to build the believability of the yarn. These folks have been so effective in their research that many urban legends passed on by email are now carrying the line, "I checked this on snopes," in the hope that you won't.

Some other very good fact checkers can be found at www.breakthechain.org, truthorfiction.com, urbanlegends.about.com and www.scambusters.org. Surf to these sites for useful, practical, and trustworthy information on identity theft, Internet scams, credit card fraud, phishing, lottery scams, urban legends, and how to stop spam. On the local level don't overlook charlottecountyfl.com/rumors where rumors of local places and issues are addressed. At the end of the site there is a place to tell the county what rumors you have heard lately. What about the fifteen story skyscraper to be built in Charlotte Harbor or the five foot long iguana seen in PGI?

For those political junkies out there try www.factcheck.org, and blog.washingtonpost.com/fact-checker. There are still more, but the point here is to do due diligence before sending on or even deciding a course of action that may be based on fantasy.

Albert Einstein said, "The important thing is not to stop questioning." Now what about those Chinese and the stock market?

DISPOSIBLE E-MAIL ACCOUNTS

Anonymity, privacy, need to know, it seems that despite laws to protect us like the HIPA form we fill out at the doctors office, every place we interact with wants information that truly isn't necessary. Example: I recently tried to download a trial version of a particular software. In order to receive the download, they wanted to know my full name, valid e-mail address, the level of my education, sex, marital status and a few other things that just aren't any of their business.

Why do they want this information? It would appear that the only use it could have would be to send **spam** to my inbox and sell the e-mails and information lists to other spammers. Granted, targeted advertising based on the information I provide, but junk mail none the less. Some of the answers can be fun. Name, I usually just pull one from what ever news article I happened to be reading or if the CEO of the company is listed on the website I'll use theirs. Education: depending on whether it is a pull down with limited choices or fields that must be filled in, I have been a kindergarten drop out to Doctor of Advanced Matriculation. For the rest of the questions I just flip a coin. But the one question that poses more of a problem is the valid e-mail. Most of these companies send a test e-mail to the account provided and if it is bounced back as a bad or non-existent account they will ask for a VALID e-mail address.

For many years now I have had an e-mail account with one of the free e-mail providers that I would provide in these situations and all the spam would go there. I rarely check this e-mail address and eventually the provider would send an e-mail to me saying that the inbox was full and if I didn't log in at least once in a while they would deactivate the account. However there is another approach available that eliminates the maintenance of a junk mail account. These are called Disposable E-mail Accounts. (DEA)

Disposable E-mail Accounts are very easy to use. Two examples of DEAs can be found at mailinator.com or www.incognitomail.com. These sites set up a temporary e-mail address that requires no password or account information to use. They have no address book, no folders, nothing but an inbox. They also don't require that we create an e-mail account with them first. For example: Imagine that we respond to an online survey by our

> **Grandma and Grandpa, how come you're so smart?**
> **Spam:** Unsolicited message transmitted via the Internet as a mass mailing to large numbers of recipients.
> It doesn't take very long for junk mail or spam to start appearing in my inbox.
> Each day I receive about twenty-five emails, five from acquaintances and twenty from spammers.
> Wrong: Hunger pangs surged when he looked at the inbox and saw all the spam.

favorite politician. At the end of the survey they want to know our e-mail address which will ensure continuing request for money, I mean more critical surveys. In the e-mail field we can put randite@mailinator.com and a test to that address will reveal it to be a real e-mail address. If we really want to see anything sent to the e-mail address, just go to mailinator.com and type in randite@mailinator.com and click check mail. This is a great way to fill in web-forms and at the same time prevent tons of spam from appearing in our real inboxes.

Better yet, there are absolutely NO signups or registrations! These accounts are completely anonymous. Any email received by DEA servers will automatically be directed to the correct inbox. There is no requirement to setup an inbox before you can receive e-mail.

Surf over to email.about.com/od/disposableemailservices/tp/disposable.htm or open a search engine and type in disposable e-mail addresses to get a list of different sites offering this service. Some temporary e-mail addresses stay active for as little as fifteen minutes or as long as twenty four hours. Pick one that serves the purpose that it is intended for. Remember these are temporary e-mail addresses and will disappear in a specified time period. If using one to actually receive information at before it disappears make sure that the service chosen will hold that e-mail address long enough to receive the requested information.

It's like having our own personal cloaking device.

PASSWORD PROTECT THE COMPUTER OR NOT?

"How do you come up with a column idea week after week?" I am asked. Don't tell anyone but most of the column ideas come from my clients. Not specifically any one of them, but when I run up against the same issue over and over, it lends itself to a column about the problem. This week we look at a **password**. Not all passwords, just one that creates problems for many folks.

The conundrum starts with the purchase of a new PC. The Windows 7 operating system is, by every measurable metric, superior to Windows XP and Vista. The initial setup is clean, straight forward and easy to accomplish. Folks have little trouble getting the new computer from the box to humming along on the Internet.

A step in the set up asks the user for a name the computer will use when booting up. The screen will display Welcome Joe or Jane. Below that a field asks for a password and a password hint lest we forget the password. This password is not for our e-mail or bank accounts, this password will allow us to acquire the desktop and our programs.

At boot up the Welcome screen asks for the password to log on to the computer. In a business environment this prevents unauthorized access to the computer or if the user leaves the computer for a time the screen saver will turn on and to regain use of the computer we need to enter the computer's password again. In a home environment having to enter a password every time can be annoying. Worse if we forget the password or the password hint doesn't trigger a recall of the correct secret code we will not be able to access the computer until we remember the correct code word.

There is the matter of grandkids, kids, neighbor kids and guests that may wish to use our computer for checking their e-mail or other purposes. For this we can password protect our user account which has administrative rights and can install or delete programs among other critical functions. We can then activate the Guest account which allows a user to access the Internet and other functions but not make any changes to our computer. To set up the Guest account click on Start – Control Panel – Users Accounts – Manage another

> **Grandma and Grandpa, how come you're so smart?**
> **Password:** A sequence of characters that must be keyed in to gain access to all or part of a computer system or program.
> Passwords should never be dictionary words, common names or other easily guessed combinations.
> A strong password is the secret to keeping our personal information private.
> Wrong: After a long journey the carrier was to password of the enemy's positions.

account. In the new window click on Guest Account. A window asks if we want to turn on the Guest account. Click Yes and the Guest account becomes active. People that do not have a user account can log onto the computer as a guest with limited privileges. They will not be able to access protected files nor make changes to the computers settings.

During a new PC set up if we leave the password request blank then no password will be required and the computer will boot directly to the desktop. Should we enter a password and decide later that we don't want it, click on Start, then Control Panel, Users Accounts and then Remove Password. It will require that we enter the old password before removal.

If we desire a password to log on to the computer it is prudent to create a Windows Password Reset Disk. To create a password reset disk, insert your removable media. Open User Accounts by clicking the Start button, clicking Control Panel, click User Accounts and in the left pane, click Create a password reset disk. Follow the instructions. Make sure you store the password reset disk in a safe place.

If no password reset disk is available and the password cannot be recalled there are still two options. Use the Recovery Disks we made after setting up the computer. This will restore the PC factory status and we can start over. This will erase all our data and files. Another option is to contact our favorite computer tech who may be able to remove the forgotten password allowing access to the computer.

Password or not, it's up to you.

PASSWORD VIGILANCE IS IMPORTANT

We all take steps to stop bad things from happening. We brush our teeth a couple times a day to prevent cavities. We cook our food to kill germs that might hurt us. We lock our homes and cars to thwart theft. We use surge protectors and battery backups to avert electrical damage to our computers, TVs and other plugged in devices. Non skid floors in bathtubs and showers are standard. Regular service on our bicycles and cars foil breakdowns at badly timed moments. It would seem natural to continue that vigilance when it comes to our online presence as well. (Martha, I think there is a lesson coming.)

Recently I have been receiving a spate of e-mails from folks I know hawking miracle drugs or products of dubious nature. Additionally e-mails arrived from concerned readers that someone they know is sending these types of e-mails to them and how can they stop this deluge of nefarious e-mails. The crux of the problem is passwords. Imperva, a data security firm, analyzed approximately 32 million passwords that had been exposed in a recent hack. From that data they posted a list of the top ten passwords used around the world. And the number one password is "123456." Safe we think, but the number four most common password is "password." And number ten is "abc123." Some of us think that because we chose a very obscure word from the dictionary we are less susceptible to being hacked, but remember hackers can use a "brute force attack" and throw an entire dictionary at the password in a matter of moments.

What does a **hacker** do with our e-mail account once it is compromised? If we're lucky, they simply send everyone in our address book a request for money, an ad for bogus products or an invitation to chat with Luscious Lucy. If we are not so lucky, they may attempt to send our entire address book a link to a virus or use our e-mail address and account to send out millions of junk emails with the sender listed as us. And even worse, once they have control of the account, they can change the password so that we can never get back in. Those of us that use free e-mail services such as Hotmail, Google or Yahoo know that it is nearly impossible if not time consuming to get help resolving these issues and sometimes the only help available is to shutdown the account and lose all the emails and addresses we had stored there. All the while we are bombarding the world with e-mail that really didn't come from us.

Grandma and Grandpa, how come you're so smart?
Hacker: Someone who breaks into computers and computer networks.
A hacker is someone that tries to break into our computer and if successful we are hacked.
A hacker can be someone that gets into our e-mail account or takes over our PC.
Wrong: George Washington took so long to chop down the cherry tree he was called a hacker.

So how can we protect ourselves from password theft? The key is tough passwords. The strength of a password depends on the different types of characters that we use, the overall length of the password, and whether the password can be found in a dictionary. It should be at least 14 characters long. Test a few of the passwords we currently use at this site. www.microsoft.com/security/pc-security/password-checker.aspx. I was surprised to find that even some of the passwords I use didn't fall into the Strong category like I thought they would. Convinced that our passwords need help, surf over to this site (www.microsoft.com/security/online-privacy/passwords-create.aspx) where Microsoft gives excellent guidelines, examples and techniques for creating tough but memorable passwords.

Here is a suggestion for creating a tough password. Choose a favorite phrase. For example; red sun at morning, sailors take warning. Use the first letter of each word and throw in a symbol, a number and a capitol letter and the password becomes very strong. Rs@mstw1 would be a very tough nut to crack but as long as we remembered our favorite saying we could recall this password when ever needed.

Let's be safe out there!

QUESTIONS FROM READERS

Did you know that only so much can be stuffed into the old e-mail bag before it explodes? Buzzers are blaring, lights are flashing, seams are tearing and the Imminent Danger sign is pulsing over the old e-mail bag. Let's relieve some of the pressure by answering a few of the more interesting e-mail questions. Time to reach in and pull out a few questions that folks have sent in. Maybe we can put some issues to rest.

Faithful reader Cathy writes, "I am a Comcast customer and downloaded and installed the Norton Antivirus package. I already had the free AVG 2011 on my computer and they seem to be "fighting" over who should be in charge. It takes sometimes up to 15 minutes for the computer to get started. Should I delete the AVG 2011 or is it better to have the two programs and just be patient while it is starting up?"

Antivirus programs are generally multi faceted programs. They contain an antivirus, antispyware, antirootkit, e-mail scanners and **firewalls**. Having more than one program on the machine would not necessarily be a problem if they were just resident and didn't run at the same time. Antivirus programs run monitors, scan downloaded files, and check emails constantly. A PC with two or more antivirus programs is consuming memory and processor resources doing the same tasks twice. Or put another way, it is taking twice as long to complete a task. Antivirus programs can actually interfere with each other, sometimes even identifying a file from the opposing program as a security threat and try to quarantine it which may result in error messages, program failure or possibly even the dreaded blue screen of death. Pick one good program and stick with it. Should we feel it necessary to run a scan with a second antivirus or antispyware program, use one of the online scanners available from many of the major antivirus companies such as Kaspersky, McAfee just to name a few. Check the program that you have loaded and if it has all the features, antivirus, antispyware, firewall etc, anything else would be redundant and a drain on the computer's performance.

Ardent reader Nancy sent this along, "All of a sudden every thing on my screen is 50% larger. Circles are ovals and everything is stretched wider. I am using Explorer and Vista Home Premium. Is there any fix that can be done quickly that you know of?

> **Grandma and Grandpa, how come you're so smart?**
> **Firewalls:** Computer software intended to prevent unauthorized access to system software or data.
> Firewalls can block everything or be fine-tuned to filter specific programs, websites, e-mails and domains.
> Two firewalls on a computer are not twice as safe but it is twice as confusing.
> Wrong: A corporate takeover of the Wall family business resulted in new management who firewalls.

It sounds like the screen resolution has changed either accidentally or perhaps because of an update to the video card. Right mouse click on an empty area of the Desktop. This opens a menu and at the bottom of the menu is the word Personalize. Click it with the left mouse button. A dialogue box will open. On the left side of the box is a link labeled Adjust Resolution. Click on it and on the next window it will display the current resolution setting. It may be something like 800X600 which was the standard resolution for the old CRT monitors. The LCD screens most folks are using can be 1024X768 or even higher depending on the monitor being used. Try some different ratios until the screen is comfortable to read. Two other points to remember, Internet Explorer 8 has in the bottom right corner the ability to magnify the screen up to 400% by clicking on the percentage and then choosing the magnification desired. Windows also has a magnifier that can be used to make reading the screen easier for those with diminished eyesight. Go to the control panel and Easy of Access Center and choose Magnifier. That pesky fine print can be elephantized in no time.

Loyal reader June writes, "I use Windows Live Mail." Lately it seems that not a single junk e-mail is going to the junk folder. Even the ones that I mark as junk reappear each day in the inbox. Is there a setting I am missing?"

Windows Live Mail is the successor to Windows Mail which succeeded Outlook Express. I use Windows Live Mail for one of my personal accounts just to have it available for troubleshooting questions like these. Until recently, like June, I liked the features and functionality of WLM even though it is a client based e-mail reader. (It resides on and runs from a personal PC, holding all the retrieved e-mail on the local machine.) I also noticed that once I had downloaded the new version, WLM 2011 it seemed that the Junk mail filter ceased to work at all.

I researched the problem at the Microsoft Support site and discovered that issue had been addressed but that to correct the problem at the user's machine required a few steps. If running WLM and the Junk Mail filter does not appear to be working, go to Control Panel – Add/Remove programs (XP) or Programs and Features (Vista and Windows 7). Find the program called Windows Live Essentials and highlight it. Now click on Uninstall/Change. A new window will appear asking if we want to remove one or all Windows Live Essential programs or Repair all Windows Live Programs. Click on repair. Windows will now repair WLM and when finished the Junk Mail filters will work as expected.

Faithful follower Meg writes, "I have a question, should I OK updates that appear for jucheck? I did not see it on my list of programs. Besides HP or Windows updates, are there others that I should expect with a blinking icon at the bottom of the screen?" What exactly is jucheck? To get the definitive answer we need to go to Java.com where jucheck is defined as follows: The jucheck.exe is the Java update verification process. This process will check on the internet for available updates for the Java software installed on your computer. If updates are available, it will notify you and/or manage the download and install of the updates. You should leave this process running in order to keep your Java up to date.

If, as a computer user, we were disciplined enough to check for a Java update on our own then we could remove jucheck. But, if we can't remember to get the oil changed in the car until long after the mileage on the reminder sticker has passed, (Martha, has he been driving your car?) it is probably prudent to leave jucheck running and accept the automatic updates from Java. As to other updates we should accept, I would recommend Windows Updates and MS Office updates, Adobe Updates, (Adobe Reader, Adobe Flash and Shockwave) some HP updates if they pertain to the function of a PC or printer. Don't forget to keep the updates current on the anti-virus program as well.

Long time reader Marilyn writes: We are thinking of getting Carbonite.com to protect our computer hard drive. Have you heard of it? Is it necessary? Carbonite is an online backup service. A small program is downloaded to the PC and then on a regular schedule this software backs up all your important data to a secure online location. Advantages are that it is automated, so it doesn't require us to remember to backup our data, secured with a password so no one but us can access it, stored off site so in the event of a major disaster our data is safe, and is accessible from any computer in the world.

Regular readers know that I have begged, pleaded, cajoled and generally made a nuisance of my self trying to convince folks to back up anything they can't afford to lose. Carbonite offers this service for $55 a year. For folks with large amounts of data this is an excellent tool. I am not endorsing Carbonite, but I am suggesting that some form of backup should be part of a computer user's regular routine. There are many companies like Carbonite, and typing online storage in any search engine will bring up lots of companies that perform this function. There are also sites like Skydrive.live.com from Microsoft that offer smaller amounts of storage space, no automation but the price is FREE. (Martha, he teases me all the time.) But for free, we must be disciplined and make sure we back up regularly.

This note from Alan. Web site http://banktracker.investigativereportingworkshop.org allows us to look up banks to see how they stack up in terms of financial stability. We can see if our bank took TARP money and how they measure up in terms of a Troubled Asset Ratio. MSNBC says this: "While it is not an official FDIC statistic, nor is it intended as a definitive predictor of the likelihood of bank failure, the troubled asset ratio apparently is a strong indicator of severe stress inside a bank because it shows the bank's ability to withstand loan losses. Of the 92 banks that have failed so far this year, 84 had troubled asset ratios of 100 percent or greater in the final quarter they reported data before they closed." How's your bank doing?

Faithful reader Joan reports that her home page has suddenly become less than full size. When she opens up Internet Explorer, any page but her home page fills the screen and the text is easy to read. But her home page is only about two thirds of the window and the text is very small. She has a brand new computer and is using IE 8. Tampa column follower Jim reports that sometimes at his age, the text on the screen when he is researching for classic car parts is so small that he just can't make it out. He asks if there is anything short of buying a larger monitor that can be done. Jim is also using Internet Explorer 8.

Fortunately for Joan and Jim a very simple fix that addresses both problems. Open Internet Explorer 8 and look at the bottom right corner of the window. There will be a tiny magnifying glass, a percentage number and a pull down arrow next to the percent sign. It is a magnifying tool for the webpage currently displayed. Click on the magnifying glass to zoom in or out or click on the pull down arrow and choices for zooming in or out from fifty percent of normal to 400% are available. Note that use of the CTRL and + or − key on the keyboard will automatically control the zoom in or out. Internet Explorer's zoom feature magnifies the entire page. Want to make just the text larger? Click on the menu item at the top of Internet Explorer labeled Page. From the dropdown menu choose Text Size and then select Larger or Largest to increase just the text size on the page, not the page itself. Both of these tools are great for reading the fine print stuck in so many documents these days. One other note, zooming in or changing the text size will not make these items print larger. That feature is controlled by the printer and every printer is different. It will take some poking around in your printer controls to find where to enlarge or reduce a document sent to the printer.

Faithful reader Charles writes in with a twofer. Court, I hope you can help me with my XP problem(s) in Outlook Express: Computer # 1: Cannot delete e-mails at all and Computer # 2: Spell check only works in French.

The issues here are primarily caused by the use of Outlook Express which has been replaced by Windows Live Mail for Windows XP and Windows Mail that ships with Windows Vista. Windows Live Mail is a FREE download from Microsoft and a very simple explanation of it would be to consider it as the new generation of Outlook Express. It looks very similar just more modern. It has all the same features of Outlook Express and adds many new features like spam controls, search etc. But back to resolving the Outlook Express issues.

When emails can no longer be deleted it indicates that the Deleted Items folder or "DBX" file is damaged. Open Outlook Express, click on Tools –Options and then click on the Maintenance tab. In that window click on Store Folder. Copy the path to the Store Folder, then close Outlook Express. Click on Start – Run and paste in the path. This will open the folder where the Deleted Items DBX file is. Highlight the Deleted Items folder, delete it and close the window. Restart Outlook Express and it creates a new Deleted Items folder and the deletion of emails will be restored.

Problem two was related to Outlook Express using the French dictionary instead of the English Dictionary. Two solutions here. One learn French. (Martha, he's kidding right?) This problem is caused by loading MS Office 2007 which uses a different dictionary format than earlier versions. Outlook Express doesn't have the ability to use this new dictionary and reverts to the French version. To resolve go to Bing, Google or your favorite search engine and look for Outlook Express spell check. This will bring up a myriad of third party dictionaries that can be installed and will allow Outlook Express to correct spelling using American English. The most popular programs are available for FREE.

Faithful reader, (name withheld out of kindness) called me this week because his computer was acting very strangely. The mouse wouldn't move, sometimes the keyboard wouldn't work and in the middle of typing an email everything would freeze. Couldn't open anything, couldn't move the mouse nothing. The PC was several years old so maybe it was time to buy a new one. He had heard that Windows Vista was a troublesome operating system. Hours spent shopping, only to find a single Windows XP machine available in the county, so he bought it. He brought the new PC home. Before he set it up however, it was suggested that he might check the BATTERIES in the wireless mouse and keyboard. New batteries and the PC acted just like new. Moral of the story is, check the batteries before calling the Computer Guru. P.S. there will still be one Windows PC available at the store after he returns it.

Loyal column maven Cathy asks, "I would like to know how much "deleting/formatting" I must do in order to not spread our lives around when we recycle this old machine?" There are many ways to handle the disposition of an older but still functional PC. If there is nothing on the machine but some pictures of Aunt Martha and some letters asking for a driveway quote then simply delete the files and let someone get a functioning PC. But perhaps there is some financial information or private correspondence better left unknown. One step to take if you have the original system recovery disks is to put them in the computer and follow the steps to format the drive and reinstall all the original software. This will put the computer's condition back the way it was when pulled from its shipping box. Not only are your personal files deleted from the computer, but the ghosts of the deleted files are written over when the new (old) software is installed. Or call a computer technician and have them do it.

Avid fan Bob writes, "Greatly enjoyed your recent column in Charlotte Sun-Herald! Also, you might have mentioned Defrag." What is Defragmentation? Defragmentation is the process of locating the noncontiguous fragments of data into which a computer file may be divided as it is stored on a hard disk, and rearranging the fragments and restoring them into fewer fragments or into the whole file. Defragmentation reduces data access time and allows storage to be used more efficiently.

I thought this was a great comment because it allows me to suggest for all the folks out there still using Windows XP that you should occasionally go to Start – All Programs – Accessories – System Tools – Defrag and run a defrag of the hard drive. When the defrag program starts, there is a button labeled Analyze, which when clicked on checks the state of fragmentation on the drive and alerts us whether we need to defrag or not. It is a long process so if we don't have to, it will save some serious time. Those of us using Windows Vista, go get some ice cream and a coffee. Vista defrags automatically and in the background so there is nothing for us to do but keep working. (Martha, not sure that is progress.)

Gordon writes, "One thing that is some what confusing to me is which is the more effective (or does it really matter). Should I add "JUNK E-MAIL" to the blocked senders list and or add senders domain to blocked senders list? Not knowing the inner workings of the web, what is the difference between domain and e-mail addresses? Is blocking a domain more effective in the long run?"

Super question. What are the differences between email addresses and a domain? Look at this email address, court@embarqmail.com. The domain that this email address belongs to is embarqmail.com. By placing my email address to the blocked senders list, your email program will no longer accept email that comes from court@embarqmail.com. However, if you block the domain embarqmail.com, email from anyone with an embarqmail.com email address will no longer be received. It would probably not be useful to block domains like embarqmail.com or Comcast.net or yahoo.com as these are used by our friends and neighbors. However, to use a real example, I just received a junk email from the domain, teethlent.net. I can block all email from this domain by entering *@teethlent.net in my blocked senders list. The asterisk is a wildcard that means that anything put in front of @teethlent.net is to be blocked. To add this to the blocked senders list in Outlook Express or Windows Mail, click on tools, message rules, blocked senders list and follow the steps to add an entry to the list.

Helen writes, "I always look forward to reading your column in the Englewood Sun, and I wondered if it's okay to turn off the power strip at the end of the day. Since I'm on cable, this would also turn off my modem. I'm sure it would save power, but would it damage the modem?"

Turning off the power to the modem poses no issues to the hardware. It might save a little on the electric bill and it will force the modem to acquire a new IP address from the Internet Service Provider every time it restarts. Again an issue of no concern.

Worry Wart Martha entreaties, "Every time I check out how much disk space I have left on my D drive for recovery, I become concerned. I have a 2008 Gateway Notebook that has 2 GB total memory. I understand that this is not much, however for a "Martha" such as I who is not a heavy time user on my domestic servant, it seems adequate for now. Currently this drive stands at 30% free or 3.88 GB free; 6.42 GB used; 10.30 GB total D space. Exactly what would I do if this drive becomes full? Is this also known as my "Hard Drive"? What kind of information is it recovering and should it be emptied, to some degree, so as to provide more space? My C Drive is 50% free if that is at all relevant.

I have done some reading on D drives but I don't trust my interpretation of what I'm reading. In essence, I don't want to mess up my computer by killing it! You're the only one I feel I can count on for a straight answer that I may comprehend.

The D drive referred to on this machine is actually the manufactures' recovery drive where all the files are stored that would be needed in the event a total recovery would be necessary to allow the PC to run properly again. The drive should not be used for storage nor should it be eliminated unless a set of recovery disks are made first. In the list of programs we will find a folder labeled something like Recovery Manager or System

Recovery Tools or maybe PC Help and Tools. In these folders will the program required to make the recovery disks. Every time we acquire a new PC, making this set of disk should be a priority.

Dale communicates, "I have a two year old eMachine desktop, out of warranty. It came with Windows Vista pre-loaded, but no software CD. There is a Windows certification label, with the Vista authentication code, fastened to the rear of the cabinet. It won't boot up. The hard drive makes a scraping sound like a cement mixer. I can install a new hard drive. But, how can I load Windows Vista without a CD?

It can't be installed without a CD. Any Vista CD that is correct for the processor you have, 32 bit or 64 bit, will work and when it asks for the product key enter the code from the sticker on your PC. Three options available, find someone with a Vista CD; hire a tech that has a Vista CD, or contact eMachines and purchase the recovery disks from them then install from that.

TO A SPEEDIER INTERNET FOR APRIL FOOLS

It's early Friday morning and I am riding my bicycle over the Collier Bridge headed towards Veterans Boulevard. I notice the bridge bike lanes, normally filled with broken glass, insulation, parts of coolers and chunks of wood from the thousands of vehicles that cross everyday are almost free of debris. As a result of a recent sweeping, my passage over the bridge that day was much easier and faster, since I didn't have to bob and weave around debris that would puncture a tire or worse.

There is the same type of problem with the Internet. In the United States there are 140 thousand terabytes moving across the Internet each month. A **terabyte** is equal to one million bytes. As they travel, bits and bytes fall by the wayside and can remain stuck in the Internet forever. Here are some statistics that lend support to that statement.

Mary Madden writing for Pew/Internet, reports their latest survey, fielded February 15 – April 6, 2006 shows that fully 73% of respondents (about 147 million adults in the US alone) are internet users.

The website About, reports there are 171 billion messages per day which means almost 2 million emails are sent every second. About 70% to 72% (or between 120 and 123 billion) of them are spam and viruses. The genuine emails are sent by around 1.1 billion email users.

An article posted by CNN says the Internet is littered with abandoned sites. There are even more dead sites that just display a 404 message. (Site not found). Don't forget the millions of ads, pop ups and other visual and audio events that occur on the web every day.

A report produced by Deloitte is claiming that we will suffer noticeable Internet bottlenecks this year. This will be due to a lack of investment in the infrastructure coupled with a growth in video traffic. Bottlenecks are likely to become apparent in some of the Internet's backbones, the terabit-capable pipes exchanging traffic between continents.

So what happens to all the email that doesn't get delivered? How can abandoned websites be allowed to take

> **Grandma and Grandpa, how come you're so smart?**
> **Terabyte:** A unit of computer data or storage space equivalent to 1,024 gigabytes or one trillion bytes.
> Most new computers today are being built with a terabyte hard drive for storing lots of photos.
> By comparison, hard drives from the late 1990's may contain two gigabytes compared to a terabyte now.
> Wrong: The geologists found evidence of terabytes fossilized in the rocks.

up precious bandwidth, server time and space? Millions of files are uploaded and downloaded from the Web every day, what happens to video downloads or uploads that don't finish? Where does all this flotsam and jetsam end up? As we attempt to maneuver the Internet, all these bits and bytes, stuck in Internet orbit around the world, work to slow down our valid Internet traffic.

Thanks to an arm of the United Nations, the International Telecommunications Union (ITU) we will be seeing some relief and hopefully a general increase in the speed with which information flows on the World Wide Web.

The ITU commissioned brilliant programmer Lirpa Sloof to lead a team in the construction of seventeen massive cyber bots. Think of these as gigantic robots but instead of being constructed of metal and electronics, the cyber bots are essentially massive programs that consist of complicated mathematical algorithms, and AI. (Artificial intelligence) It will be the responsibility of these cyber bots to travel over the entire Internet in a twenty-four hour period, scrubbing dead websites, email, broken links, failed up and down loads etc. To enable these 'bots" to effectively clean the Internet, the United Nations has divided the world into project areas assigned to specific groups so the cyber bots can be tracked and areas deemed cleansed before they move on to the next. Our region falls under a group called the Authorized Protocol Routing for Internet Laundering.

To facilitate this Internet cleaning, the United Nations has issued a directive that will cause the Internet to be completely shut down from midnight March 31, 2008 to 12:01 a.m. April 2, 2008. Additionally, it is recommended that all computers with Internet access be shut off as well, to prevent the chance that cyber bots might enter a computer and wipe it clean if dead or unused material were found.

As each cyber bot completes an assigned project area, another group of scientist will undertake a verification and inspection of each cleaned area. This group, named the Final Overview of Operational Links and Systems will then certify the success of the cyber bots.

Since the Internet will be down during this period, I look forward to the traditional print media keeping us apprised of the progress and success of the cyber bots. I am sure that the two groups responsible for this massive undertaking, Authorized Priority Routing for Internet Laundering (A.P.R.I.L) and Final Overview of Operational Links and Systems (F.O.O.L.S) will release regular progress reports.

Here's to a faster Internet.

BOO BYTES FOR HALLOWEEN COMPUTER GHOULS

I always like the last few months of the year. The holidays are stacked up one right after another. Halloween, Thanksgiving, Christmas, New Years Eve and New Years Day bring time off for lots of parties, tons of food and fun. With Halloween just a few days off, surely our binary buddy can find us a few interesting tidbits to scare up a really good time.

Start by surfing over to en.**wikipedia**.org/wiki/Halloween for the history of Halloween. Here we can find out about the origin of the word Halloween, the symbols of the holiday and even the origin of "trick or treat." With our inquisitive nature filled use the browser to navigate to allrecipes.com/Recipes/holidays-and-events/halloween/tricks-and-treats. Recipes to haunt any party are listed here if you dare. Need still more? Type Halloween Recipes in any search engine and spend the rest of the night over a hot cauldron.

Headed to a party? Need a costume that will haunt your friends? Take a look at www.coolest-homemade-costumes.com. Here are hundreds of ideas for inexpensive but amazing home made costumes for that special night under the moon.

But surely our calculating construct would like to join in the festivities. If we are running Windows XP use the web to visit www.themesunlimited.com/Halloween.asp. Click on the list of desktop backgrounds on the left and preview it on the right. Find the one that suits the mood and click on download this site and save it to the desktop. Now double click on the file to install the scary theme to the desktop's background. Running Vista? Take a look at windows.microsoft.com/en-US/windows/downloads/personalize/wallpaper-desktop-background and download a terrifying background theme for our digital domestique. Those of us using Windows 7 can find our way to windows.microsoft.com/en-US/windows/downloads/personalize/themes to install the latest terrifying desktop themes from our friends at Microsoft.

Now that our data dynamo is dressed for the season we can cue the scary music. Use any search engine such as Bing, Google or Yahoo and type scary Halloween music in the search field. Thousands of sites offering all types of terrifying sounds will be found. Try www.mediafire.com/?ltnktunymuk for a sound track that can be

---

Grandma and Grandpa, how come you're so smart?
Wikipedia: A free, web-based, collaborative, multilingual encyclopedia project.
Wikipedia is a term coined by combining the Hawaiian Wiki (quick) and encyclopedia.
Over 100000 people world wide contribute to Wikipedia as a collaborative effort open to all.
Wrong: The scientist noted the new multi legged creature and called it a Wikipedia.

looped (plays over and over) in Windows Media Player or our favorite player.

For even more fun, set a monitor in the window beside the front door and go to youtu.be/o6T0ZnBnQUQ. This is the YouTube video that goes with the scary music and the effect is chilling. Those little rug rats ringing the doorbell on Halloween will be shaking in their boots.

What Halloween would be complete without a scary computer story for the dark of night? A story sure to make the hair on our neck stand up straight? Goosebumps no charge. Here is one from a column that set my binary buddies hard drive lights flashing when I read it to them.

BLUE SCREEN OF DEATH!

The night wore on as I sat working quietly in my office, ten o'clock, eleven o'clock and later still. Through the window, the cloud covered sky obscured any trace of star or moon. Darkness hung like a thick night shade. Working only by the soft luminescence of the computer screens in my office, I was unaware of the hour and the time slipping by. Perhaps it was the gentle, monotonous tick tock of the clock on the wall that drew me deeper and deeper into my work and further away from the mundane world of a computer tech. Or it might have been the warm comfortable symbiosis with the machines in my office that pulled my consciousness away from the logic and solidity of the real world. These computers, that had served me well and without complaint, one for more than a year, the other just a year, were like old and trusted friends.

Like a black cat skulking from the corner of the office came a rhythmic sound. Barely audible at first, it gradually became louder and louder. I turned to see where the noise was emanating from and realized it was coming from the second and youngest computer. What could it be? It began to imitate a heartbeat as it continued to grow louder still. Ka-thump, ka-thump, this wasn't right, it wasn't machine like. I reached for the mouse, hoping to open the volume control and mute the noise while I searched for the cause. At the touch of my hand to the mouse the cursor began to fly around the screen, going where it wished, ignoring my input. Windows and dialog boxes opened and closed of their own volition. The task bar at the bottom of the desktop jumped to the top of the screen, then to the sides and finally to triple its normal width before disappearing altogether. And still louder, KA-thump, KA-thump.

Now I began to worry about my old friend. What was causing these anomalies? Surely this was but a minor glitch, (a common technical term) and nothing to worry about. Often the best solution is to reset and reboot. Since the mouse now had a mind of its own, I reached down and pushed the power button once, which with Windows XP begins the shut down process. The monitor screen began to dim, as if to sleep. Nevertheless, louder came the KA-Thump, KA-Thump.

Suddenly the screen flared brightly, and still more windows and dialog boxes opened and closed at a kaleidoscopic pace. Instead of shutting down, the computer was now out of control, performing acts that surely were causing distress to its electronic soul. Still hoping to find a cause, I reverted to keyboard commands in a desperate attempt to access the internet where perhaps an antidote could be found. Internet Explorer opened its portal to the web and a chill streaked down my spine as a blindingly white page opened with the horrible pronouncement, "The Page Cannot Be Displayed." I feared for the existence of my PC compatriot. KA-THUmp, KA-THUmp.

Could the old technician's tales of computer gremlins be true? Something had stolen my computer's identity from me. Were these gremlins destroying my mechanical friend, or simply toying with me in some cruel and despicable way? If gremlins did exist then they must leave a trail in the Task Manager. Without hesitation, I hit the CTRL, ALT and Delete keys to open the Task Manager. Anxiously I searched for some telltale heart that didn't belong. As if to warn me to cease my efforts the ominous sounds increase ever more. KA-THUMp, KA-THUMp.

Finally, with an ear splitting KA-THUMP, KA-THUMP, I reached down and pushed the power button in and held it there. This was the mercy kill. In five or six seconds my calculating servant would enjoy sweet oblivion and respite from these torments. But the beast or fiends that held my PC as their thrall were not done yet. One last attempt to spread fear was displayed on the screen. Something I have not seen for sometime. The ominous, Blue Screen of Death. Then all went black and the sounds of torment ceased.

Happy Halloween.

NIGHT BEFORE CHRISTMAS IN COMPUTERLAND

Twas the night before Christmas when all through the house,
Lights flashed on the tower and even the mouse.
The Webcams were ready, installed with great care.
In hopes that grandkids would be virtually there.

The children were nestled all snug in their beds,
While visions of computer games danced in their heads;
Mamma in her rocker, a netbook on her lap.
To check Santa's route on Norads' tracking map.

Last minute shopping, I knew it would matter,
Receipts from the printer were spit with a clatter.
The e-mail program began to beep and flash,
Away to the desktop I flew in a dash,
An e-mail from Santa, I pulled from the cache.

The sleigh was loaded, the springs sitting low
Boxes of computer games, only kids know.
Dead Space II for Tommy, Pokemon for Sue,
Xbox, Wii, Playstation and Nintendo too.

Neither Mamma nor I had Santa forgot,
A wireless keyboard and mouse in the lot.
From a webcam mounted some far away place
An image so small, across the screen it did race.

What could it be I wondered, what would appear,
But a miniature sleigh, and eight tiny reindeer,
With a little old driver, so lively and quick,
I knew in a moment it must be St. Nick.

I toggled the volume and turned it up loud
As his digital facade flew over the clouds

At the speed of Moore's law his coursers they came,
And he whistled, and shouted, and called them by name;
"Now, Dell! now, Gates! now, Jobs and Wosniak!
On, Bezos! on Ellison! on, Hewlett and Packard!
To the top of the toolbar! The top of the screen!

Now pixels are changing, amazed by it all!
The picture expanded as closer he drew
His exact location surely only he knew.
But Google Street view offered a hopeful clue.
Just a click of the mouse, our house was in view.

With the sleigh full of downloads, upgrades and such
St. Nicholas too, might it be just too much?
The broadband was humming the router secure
A shiny new computer I'm sure will allure

Firewalls open for the jolly red elf.
Presents are coming, surely some for myself.
And then, in a twinkling, I heard on the roof
The prancing and pawing of each little hoof.

A mystery for sure I pondered aloud.
Could Santa be real an answer I vowed.
An Internet search for the jolly St. Nick
"Santa Claus: could he be real" should turn the trick

Pages and pages of results did appear
To read them all might take 'til Christmas next year.
My eyelids grew heavy then started to droop,
A short nap was needed so I could regroup.

Foggy and confused from my slumber I stirred,
"You've got mail," from the speakers I heard.
An e-mail from Santa's own Smartphone it said,
A tight schedule barred his waking me he pled.
Presents for all under the tree he had spread.
Click here for a live video feed of the sled.

The digital image danced and sparkled bright.
Santa driving his sleigh on it's magical flight.
But I heard him exclaim, ere he drove out of sight,
"Merry Christmas to all, and to all a good-night."

VOCABULARY APPENDIX

Website	User ID	Passwords	Notes

ABOUT THE AUTHOR

Courtland Nederveld was born a very small child in Grand Rapids, Michigan. Currently living in Charlotte County, located in sunny southwest Florida. After spending thirteen years with corporate information technology he seized the opportunity to move on. Continuing with computer consulting he also began to pen short travel and humor articles for the local newspaper. Encouraged to tackle writing a how to weekly PC column in 2004 for the community, his Bits and Bytes byline quickly became a weekly staple. Other published work includes, On the Road series, Great American Pony Drive, and Epicuria: Adventures That Really Cook! Short stories include Earth's Last Twelve Hours, Harlequin, The Studier Becomes the Studied, My Other Half and The End of the Beginning.